Cells – structure fits function

Imagine that you can travel back through time to 1665 – which i[s]
when the English scientist Robert Hooke first described the simple
box-like shapes that he saw down his early microscope as cells.
Imagine explaining to him that his simple cells are in reality highly
complex structures, like the one shown on the cover, and that they are
hives of activity.

There is no doubt that all organisms, from a single-celled bacterium
to an elephant, are made of cells, but these cells are not simply
building blocks. Cells like nerve cells, sperm cells and blood cells are
highly specialised structures with specific functions. And to make the
body even more efficient, cells are organised into tissues and systems
that work together.

All cells are incredibly busy generating energy through the process
of respiration. There are materials coming into and out of the cell by
the processes of diffusion and osmosis. Cells manufacture molecules;
they carry molecules and information around the body; they
defend the body against invaders; they provide structure and
the means for movement.

Imagine what you might tell Hooke about genes
and DNA and how modern-day scientists have not
only discovered the molecular structure of DNA,
but can manipulate individual bases within DNA in
the exciting new world of genetic engineering.

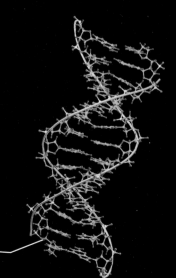

DNA

William Collins' dream of knowledge for all began with the publication of his first book in 1819. A self-educated mill worker, he not only enriched millions of lives, but also founded a flourishing publishing house.

Today, staying true to this spirit, Collins books are packed with inspiration, innovation and practical expertise. They place you at the centre of a world of possibility and give you exactly what you need to explore it.

Collins
DO MORE

Published by Collins
An imprint of HarperCollinsPublishers
77–85 Fulham Palace Road,
Hammersmith,
London W6 8JB

Browse the complete Collins Education catalogue at
www.collinseducation.com

©HarperCollinsPublishers Limited 2006

10 9 8 7 6 5 4 3 2

ISBN-10: 0-00-775546-5
ISBN-13: 978-0-00-775546 2

Jackie Clegg, Gareth Price and Mike Smith assert their moral right
to be identified as the authors of this work

British Library Cataloguing in Publication Data
A Catalogue record for this publication is available from the British
Library

New text by Kate Turner Haig
Edited by Kay Macmullan
Cover design by White-Card, London
Text page design by Sally Boothroyd
New artwork by Jerry Fowler

Printed and bound by Printing Express, Hong Kong

This high quality material is endorsed by Edexcel and has been through a rigorous quality assurance programme to ensure that it is a suitable companion to the specification for both learners and teachers.
This does not mean that its contents will be used verbatim when setting examinations nor is it to be read as being the official specification – a copy of which is available at **www.edexcel.org.uk**

Acknowledgements:
The Authors and Publishers are grateful to the following for
permission to reproduce copyright material:

Edexcel Ltd: pp 128–154
Edexcel Ltd accept no responsibility whatsoever for the accuracy or
method of working in the answers given.

Photographs
Holt Studios International 107; Jupiterimages Corporation © 2006
9 (R), 9 (B), 26, 34, 45, 46, 50, 60, 79, 117, 119, 120, 170–173; Andrew
Lambert 87, 123 (T); Wally McNamee/Corbis 43; Ian Pritchard 112;
Science Photo Library 56, 88, 108, 123 (B); David Vincent 4 (L), 4 (C),
18 (T), 18 (C), 28, 96, 113 (T), 113 (C)

Cover: Getty Images, Dr George Chapman

Inside Front Cover spread: red blood cells – Eye of Science/Science
Photo Library; nerve cells – BSIP, Joubert/Science Photo Library;
sperm cells – Eye of Science/Science Photo Library; DNA molecule –
Pasieka/Science Photo Library

Section spreads: pp6/7 bumble bee bat – Merlin Tuttle/Science
Photo Library; pp12/13 heart – BO Veisland/Science Photo Library;
pp74/75 yeast cells – Astrid & Hanns-Frieder Michler/Science Photo
Library; pp94/95 rafflesia flower – Georgette Douwma/Science Photo
Library; pp110/111 Coloured SEM of 5 different types of rice grain –
Eye of Science/Science Photo Library

Every effort has been made to contact the holders of copyright
material, but if any have been inadvertently overlooked, the
Publishers will be pleased to make the necessary arrangements at
the first opportunity.

IGCSE for Edexcel

BIOLOGY

by Jackie Clegg, Gareth Price
& Mike Smith

Collins

GETTING THE BEST FROM THE BOOK

Welcome to *IGCSE Biology for Edexcel*. This textbook and the accompanying CD-ROM have been designed to help you understand all of the requirements needed to succeed in the Edexcel IGCSE Biology course. Just as there are five sections in the Edexcel syllabus so there are five sections in the textbook: The nature and variety of living organisms; Structures and functions in living organisms; Reproduction and inheritance; Ecology and the environment and Use of biological resources. Each section in the book covers the essential knowledge and skills you need. The textbook also has some very useful features that have been designed to help you understand all the aspects of Biology that you will need to know for this specification.

Coverage of each topic is linked closely to the Edexcel specification so that you build a powerful knowledge-base with which to succeed in the examination.

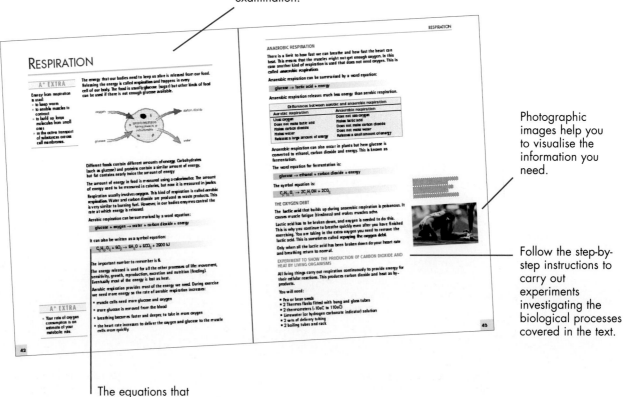

Photographic images help you to visualise the information you need.

Follow the step-by-step instructions to carry out experiments investigating the biological processes covered in the text.

The equations that you need to know are given in both word and symbol form.

There will be two stages to your assessment on the course because Edexcel IGCSE Biology is assessed in the following manner:

Paper 1 – Examination 1F – The Foundation Tier, worth 80% of the marks.

OR

Paper 2 – Examination 2H – The Higher Tier, worth 80% of the marks.

AND

Paper 3 – Examination 3 - common to both tiers, worth 20% of the marks

OR

Paper 4 – Coursework – common to both tiers, worth 20% of the marks.

Collins *IGCSE Biology for Edexcel* covers all of the topics and skills you will need to achieve success, whichever assessment pathway you are entered for.

Clear illustrations help you to understand biological processes and structures.

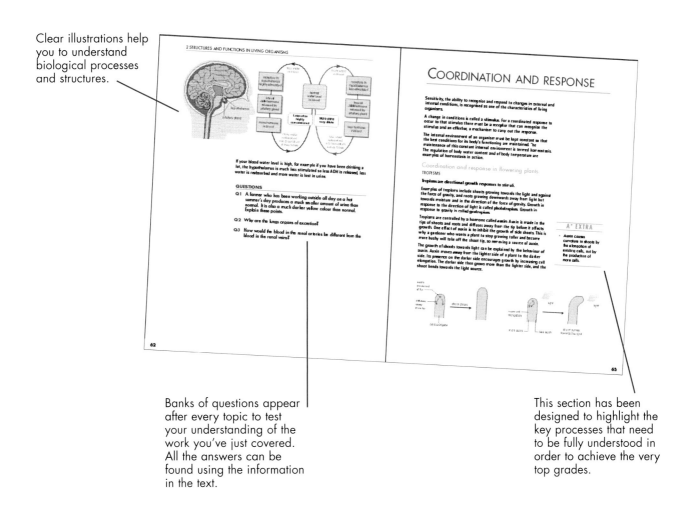

Banks of questions appear after every topic to test your understanding of the work you've just covered. All the answers can be found using the information in the text.

This section has been designed to highlight the key processes that need to be fully understood in order to achieve the very top grades.

IGCSE Biology CD-ROM

To help you through the course we have added a unique CD-ROM which may be used in class or by yourself as part of your private study. To allow you to really understand the subject as you progress through the course we have added the following features to the CD-ROM:

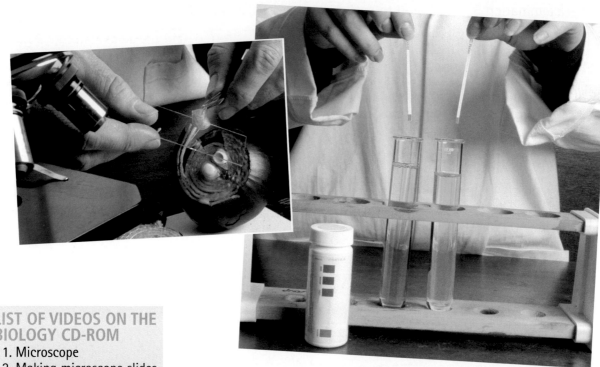

VIDEO CLIPS

Biology is a practical subject and to reinforce your studies the CD-ROM includes 19 short films that demonstrate experiments and practical work. Each of the films covers an area that you need to know well for the practical section of the course. The information in the films will also help you with the knowledge required in other parts of the specification. You can use the films to help you understand the topic you are currently studying or perhaps come back to them when you want to revise for the exam.

Each of the films has sound too, so if you are watching them in a library or quiet study area you may need headphones.

QUESTION BANK

'Practice makes perfect', the saying goes, and we have included a large bank of questions related to the Biology syllabus to help you understand the topics you will be studying.

As with the films, your teacher may use this in class or you may want to try the questions in your private study sessions.

These questions will reinforce the knowledge you have gained in the classroom and through using the textbook and could also be used when you are revising for your examinations. Don't try to do all the questions at once though; the most effective way to use this feature is by trying some of the questions every now and then to test yourself. In this way you will know where you need to do a little more work. The questions are not full 'exam-type' questions that you will be set by your IGCSE examiners. Some of the questions test underlying principles thatare not specifically mentioned in your specification.

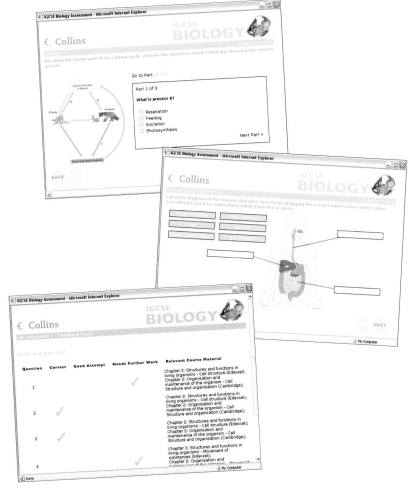

Good luck with your IGCSE Biology studies. This book and the CD-ROM provide you with stimulating, interesting and motivating learning resources that we are sure will help you succeed in your biology course.

OPERATING SYSTEMS REQUIRED AND SET-UP INSTRUCTIONS.

Mac System requirements

500 MHz PowerPC G3 and later
Mac OS X 10.1.x and above
128MB RAM
Microsoft Internet Explorer 5.2, Firefox 1.x, Mozilla 1.x, Netscape 7.x and above, Opera 6, or Safari 1.x and above (Mac OS X 10.2.x only)
325 MB of free hard disc space.

To run the program from the CD

1 Insert the CD into the drive
2 When the CD icon appears on the desktop, double-click it
3 Double-click Collins IGCSE Biology.html

To install the program to run from the hard drive

1 Insert the CD into the drive
2 When the CD icon appears on the desktop, double-click it to open a finder window
3 Drag Collins IGCSE Biology.html to the desktop
4 Drag Collins IGCSE Biology Content to the desktop.

PC System requirements

450 MHz Intel Pentium II processor (or equivalent) and later
Windows 98/ME/NT/2000/XP
128MB RAM
Microsoft Internet Explorer 5.5, Firefox 1.x, Mozilla 1.x, Netscape 7.x and above, Opera 7.11 and above
325 MB of hard disc space

To run the program from the CD

1 Insert the CD into the drive
2 Double-click on the CD-ROM drive icon inside My Computer
3 Double-click on Collins IGCSE Biology.html

To install the program to run from the hard drive

1 Insert the IGCSE Biology disc into your CD-ROM drive
2 Double-click on the CD-ROM drive icon inside My Computer
3 Double-click on the SETUP.EXE
4 Follow onscreen instructions. These include instructions concerning the Macromedia Flash Player included with and required by the program.
5 When the installation is complete, remove the CD from the drive.

For free technical support, call our helpline on: Tel.: + 44 141 306 3322 or send an email to: it.helpdesk@harpercollins.co.uk.

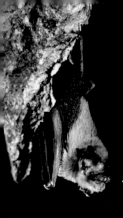

The bumblebee bat (*Craseonycteris thonglongyai*) is thought to be the smallest mammal in the world, weighing about the same as a bumblebee. It feeds on insects, and has a combined head and body length of only 3 centimetres (reproduced here at its original size)

Variety is the spice of life

Southeast Asia has some of the most biodiverse, or species-rich, regions on Earth. The tropical rainforests alone are home to a huge diversity of mammals, ranging from elephants through to the miniscule bumblebee bat (thought to be the smallest mammal in the world); numerous birds (Peninsular Malaysia alone has some 650 species), over 100 species of snake, crocodiles and other amphibians. And there's a vast array of insect life, including many stunningly beautiful butterflies. Plant life ranges from the Rafflesia species, with the world's largest flowers, through to carnivorous pitcher plants and tiny mosses.

Chapter 1

THE NATURE AND VARIETY OF LIVING ORGANISMS

CHARACTERISTICS OF LIVING ORGANISMS

Almost all living things (**organisms**) are made up of building blocks called **cells**. Most cells are so small that they can only be seen with a microscope.

Cells help organisms carry out some of the processes that are vital for life. There are seven processes needed for life:

- Movement – in all living cells protoplasm moves, in more complex organisms the whole structure may move. Animals can move their entire bodies; plants may move in response to external stimuli, such as light.

- Respiration – respiration is a process that transfers energy using chemical reactions in living organisms; cells are able to bring about chemical reactions by which energy is released for their own purposes.

- Sensitivity – living things are able to recognise and respond to changes in their external and internal conditions.

- Growth – in growth the amount of protoplasm within a cell may be increased or, in multicellular organisms, the number of cells may increase.

- Reproduction – living organisms are able to increase their numbers and so maintain their species.

- Excretion – this is the process by which an organism eliminates the waste products of its chemical activities.

- Nutrition – this is the intake of materials necessary for energy release, for growth, and for the manufacture of secretory substances.

An easy way to remember all seven processes is to take the first letter from each process. This spells Mrs Gren. Alternatively you may wish to make up a sentence in which each word begins with same letter as one of the processes, for example, My Revision System Gets Really Entertaining Now.

More questions on the CD ROM

QUESTIONS

Q1 Can you remember the seven processes of life? Try making up your own sentence to help you.

Q2 Name two life processes necessary for an organism to release energy.

Answers are on page 158.

VARIETY OF LIVING ORGANISMS

Living organisms come in a wide variety of forms. Modern biology classifies living organisms on the basis of their structure and how they function. This means that we can divide organisms into different groups.

Plants

Plants are multicellular organisms.

Plant cells have a **cell wall** as well as a cell membrane. The cell wall is made of **cellulose** and gives the cell shape and support.

A plant cell's **vacuole** contains a liquid called cell sap, which is water with various substances dissolved in it for storage. In a healthy plant the vacuole is large and helps support the cell.

Plants contain chloroplasts and are able to carry out photosynthesis, a process in which they use the Sun's energy to produce carbohydrates. Carbohydrates are stored as starch or sucrose. These are used to store energy for the plant but can also be used as food by animals that eat plants.

Plants vary greatly in size and shape, from tall rainforest trees to tiny flowers like the violet. We use many plants as food, including cereals such as rice and maize, and herbaceous legumes such as lentils, peas and beans.

Animals

Animals are muticellular organisms. Unlike plants they do not contain chloroplasts and so cannot carry out photosynthesis. They have to utilise other organisms (plants or other animals) as food. They have a cell membrane but no cell wall. Many animals are able to coordinate their movement using nerves and are able to travel from one place to another. Carbohydrates are stored by animals for energy, often in the form of glycogen.

As with plants, the variety of animals is huge, from enormous whales and elephants to tiny ants.

Fungi

Some fungi are single-celled but most fungi have a structure consisting of fine threads known as hyphae. Each hypha may contain many nuclei. Several hyphae together form a mycelium. Many fungi can be seen without a microscope. Their cell walls are made of chitin, a fibrous carbohydrate. They are similar to plants but have no chlorophyll. This means that they cannot carry out photosynthesis. To obtain energy they secrete digestive enzymes onto organic food material from plants or animals and absorb nutrients. This is called saprotrophic nutrition. Like animals, they may store carbohydrate in the form of glycogen.

Examples of fungi include yeast, a single-celled fungus used by humans in baking and brewing, and *Mucor*, a fungus with the typical hyphal structure. *Mucor* is often seen as a mould growing on spoiled foods.

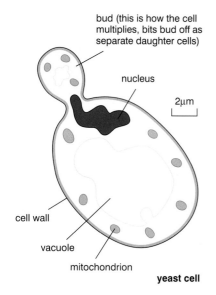

yeast cell

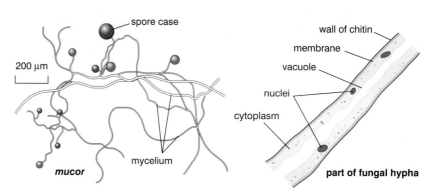

mucor

part of fungal hypha

Bacteria

Bacteria are microscopic single-celled organisms. They can be seen with a light microscope. They have no proper nucleus but contain a circular chromosome of DNA. Some bacteria are able to photosynthesise but most have to obtain nutrients by feeding off other organisms. Most bacteria reproduce asexually by binary fission (splitting into two). If conditions are unfavourable bacteria can produce spores, which are resistant to variations in temperature and pH.

Some bacteria are useful to humans, for example *Lactobacillus bulgaricus*, a rod-shaped bacterium used to make yoghurt. Other bacteria are pathogens, causing diseases in plants and animals. An example of a pathogen is *Pneumococcus*, a spherical bacterium that can cause pneumonia.

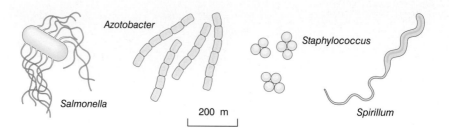

Viruses

Viruses are even smaller than bacteria. They cannot be seen with a light microscope, only with an electron microscope. Viruses are parasitic and can only reproduce inside the living cells of another organism. For this reason some people say that viruses are not 'living'. They consist of a protein coat surrounding genetic information either in the form of DNA or RNA. In order to reproduce, viruses have to 'infect' another organism. There are viruses that can infect every type of living thing.

The tobacco mosaic virus is a plant virus. It causes discolouring of the leaves of tobacco plants by preventing the formation of chloroplasts.

Influenza viruses are a group of many closely related viruses that can cause 'flu' in many different animals including humans.

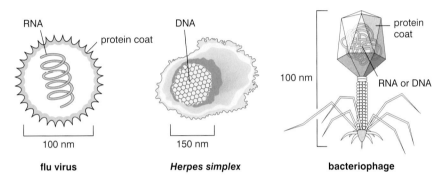

| flu virus | *Herpes simplex* | bacteriophage |

```
1 m = 1000 mm (millimetres)
1 mm = 1000 μm (micrometres)
1 μm = 1000 nm (nanometres)
```

QUESTIONS

Q1 Give two differences between plants and animals.

Q2 What is special about the way in which viruses reproduce?

Q3 Name two groups of living organisms that use glycogen as an energy store.

More questions on the CD ROM

Answers are on page 158.

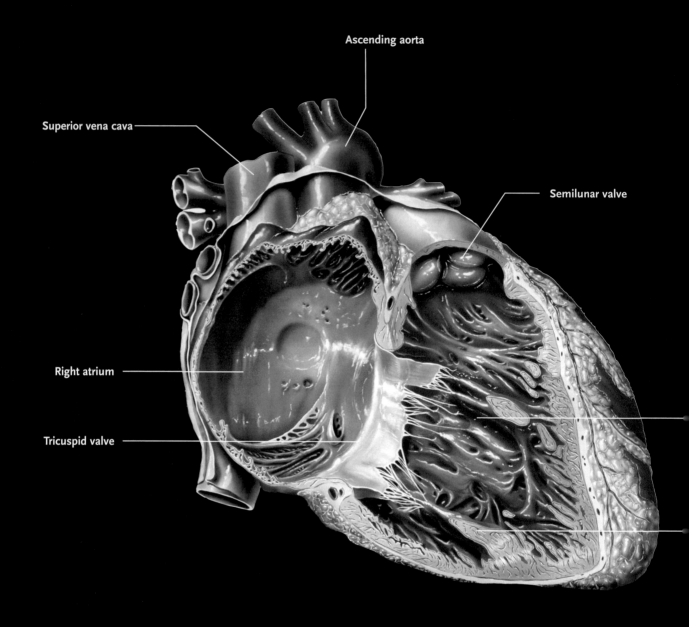

Ascending aorta

Superior vena cava

Semilunar valve

Right atrium

Tricuspid valve

The heart of the matter

The beating of the heart and breathing are described as vital signs – they show that a person is alive. And to stay alive, your body, and particularly your brain, needs oxygen for respiration. You breathe in oxygen in air. Oxygen diffuses from the alveoli in the lungs into red blood cells. The heart pumps the blood around the body, delivering oxygen to every single cell. Oxygen also reaches the cells by the simple process of diffusion: it moves from an area of high concentration to an area of low concentration. So here it moves from the red blood cells into tissues.

Chapter 2

STRUCTURES AND FUNCTIONS IN LIVING ORGANISMS

Left ventricle

Papillary muscle

LEVELS OF ORGANISATION

Cells

The cells that make up organisms all have certain things in common. Each cell is surrounded by a cell membrane, inside which is a jelly-like substance called the cytoplasm. Within the cytoplasm are structures called **organelles**. The most obvious organelle is usually the nucleus, containing the cell's genetic material. Other organelles, such as mitochondria and chloroplasts, carry out some of the cell's reactions.

Tissues

Some organisms are unicellular and some possess only a few cells. In larger organisms, which may have millions of cells, some of the cells are specialised and are organised into tissues. Muscle cells, for example, are specially adapted to create movement and are arranged in large groups to create muscle tissue; nerve cells transmit messages from one to another and are organised into nervous tissue such as the brain, spinal cord and nerves.

Organs

Organs are structures within large organisms that are adapted to doing a specific function. The function of the stomach is to digest food. To do this it has tissues that perform different tasks. Secretory tissue lining the stomach produces enzymes to break down the food; muscle tissue in the wall of the stomach churns up the food to mix it with the enzymes and moves the food through the stomach. These actions are controlled by nerves to the stomach.

Systems

Organs like the stomach form part of larger structures called systems. The stomach is part of the digestive system. The digestive system has many parts other than the stomach, including the teeth, the oesophagus and the intestines.

Together organelles form cells; specialised cells are grouped together to form tissues; different tissues come together to form organs; organs are arranged in systems; and the systems make up the whole organism.

CELL STRUCTURE

Plant cells have features that are not found in animal cells.
The diagrams below show a typical animal cell and typical plant cells.

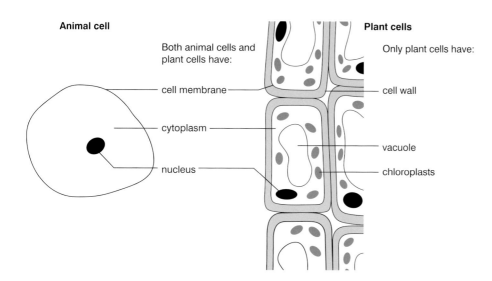

Animal cell

Both animal cells and plant cells have:

- cell membrane
- cytoplasm
- nucleus

Plant cells

Only plant cells have:

- cell wall
- vacuole
- chloroplasts

The **cell membrane** holds the cell together and controls substances entering and leaving the cell. A plant cell also has a cell wall made of cellulose giving the cell extra support and defining its shape.

The **cytoplasm** is more complicated than it looks. It is where many different chemical processes happen. The cytoplasm contains **enzymes** that control these chemical processes. In the cytoplasm of plant cells there is a large **vacuole** containing cell sap. The vacuole is used for storage and to support the shape of the cell. If the plant is healthy the vacuole will be full. If there is not enough sap in the vacuole the cell will tend to collapse.

The **nucleus** contains **chromosomes** and **genes**. These control how a cell grows and works. Genes also control the features that can be passed on to offspring.

Plant cells also contain **chloroplasts**. These contain the green pigment **chlorophyll**, which absorbs the light energy that plants need to make food in the process known as **photosynthesis**.

Similarities	Differences	
Both animal and plant cells contain	**Animal cells**	**Plant cells**
Cell membrane	Have no cell wall	Have a cell wall
Cytoplasm	Have no large vacuole (although	Usually have a large vacuole
Nucleus	there may be small temporary vacuoles)	
	Have no chloroplasts	Green parts of a plant contain chloroplasts
	Have many irregular shapes	Usually have a regular shape

QUESTIONS

Q1 Look at the diagram of an onion cell.

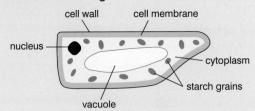

a How is the onion cell different from a typical plant cell?
b Explain the reason for this difference.
c How is the onion cell different from an animal cell?

Q2 Name which part of a cell does the following.
a Allows oxygen to enter.
b Contains the genes.
c Contains cell sap.
d Stops plant cells swelling if they take in a lot of water.

More questions on the CD ROM

Q3 How do plants obtain energy for photosynthesis?

Answers are on page 158.

BIOLOGICAL MOLECULES

Videos & questions
on the CD ROM

Most of the molecules found in living organisms fall into three groups: carbohydrates, proteins and lipids (fats and oils). All of these molecules contain carbon, hydrogen and oxygen. In addition proteins contain nitrogen.

Carbohydrate molecules are made up of small sub-units called sugars. Sugars are made from carbon, hydrogen and oxygen atoms arranged in a ring-shaped molecule. Groups of sugar molecules can link together to make larger molecules and long-chain polymers called polysaccharides, e.g. starch.

Protein molecules are made up of long chains of amino acids linked together.

Lipid molecules are made up of the trihydric alcohol glycerol linked to fatty acids.

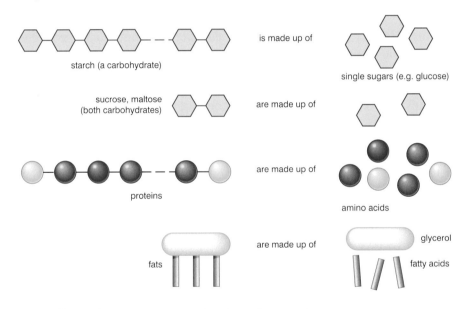

starch (a carbohydrate) is made up of single sugars (e.g. glucose)

sucrose, maltose (both carbohydrates) are made up of

proteins are made up of amino acids

fats are made up of glycerol / fatty acids

Basic units of carbohydrates, proteins and fats.

Tests for glucose, starch, lipids and protein

The following simple tests can be used to test foods for the presence of starch, reducing sugars, protein or fat.

GLUCOSE (REDUCING SUGAR)

Glucose is a 'reducing sugar' and its presence can be detected using Benedict's reagent. If a precipitate forms when the Benedict's solution is added to a prepared sample containing the glucose, and heated to 95°C, this indicates the presence of reducing sugars. If there is a significant amount of sugar present the precipitate will be an orange-red colour. A green colour means only a small amount of sugar.

STARCH

When iodine solution is mixed with starch it changes from brown to dark blue. This happens when even small amounts of starch are present and can be used as a simple test for the presence of starch. The sample to be

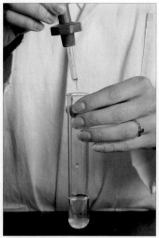

Protein test – before

Protein test – after

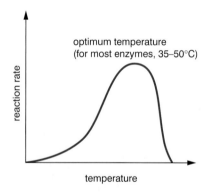

optimum temperature
(for most enzymes, 35–50°C)

reaction rate

temperature

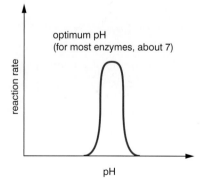

optimum pH
(for most enzymes, about 7)

reaction rate

pH

Enzymes work best at an optimum temperature and optimum pH.

tested can be ground up and mixed with distilled water. A few drops of iodine solution are then added to the sample. A blue-black colour indicates the presence of starch. This is easiest to see if the test is examined against a white background.

LIPIDS

This test depends upon the fact that lipids do not dissolve in water but will in ethanol. The test sample is mixed with ethanol. If lipid is present it will be dissolved in the ethanol to form a solution. The liquid formed is poured into a test tube of water, leaving behind any solid that has not dissolved. If there is any lipid dissolved in the ethanol it will form a cloudy white precipitate when mixed with the water.

PROTEIN

The Biuret test is used to check for the presence of protein. A small sample is placed in a test tube. An equal volume of Biuret solution is carefully poured down the side of the tube. If the sample contains protein a blue ring forms at the surface. If the sample is then shaken the blue ring will disappear and the solution will turn a light purple.

ENZYMES

Enzymes are proteins that act as biological catalysts controlling the rate of metabolic reactions in living organisms.

Enzymes are produced by cells.

Enzymes help chemical substances change into new substances.

Enzymes are **specific**, which means that each enzyme only works on one substance.

Enzymes work best at a particular temperature (around 35–40°C for human digestive enzymes), called their **optimum temperature**. At temperatures that are too high the structure of an enzyme will be changed so that it will not work. This is irreversible and the enzyme is said to be **denatured**.

Enzymes work best at a particular pH, called their **optimum pH**. Extremes of (very high or very low) pH can also denature enzymes.

EXPERIMENT TO SHOW THE EFFECT OF TEMPERATURE ON ENZYME ACTIVITY

Developed black and white negative film consists of a celluloid backing covered with a layer of gelatin. Where the film has been exposed the gelatin layer contains tiny particles of silver which make that area black. Gelatin is a protein and is easily digested by enzymes called proteases.

You will need:
- 5 test tubes
- 5 water baths set at 10°C, 20°C, 30°C, 40°C and 50°C
- Lengths of exposed and developed 35mm black and white film
- Scissors
- Stopwatch or clock
- Suitable protease solution

1 Cut the film into strips and place one in each of the five tubes.

2 Add 10ml of protease solution to the tubes and place one in each of the water baths. Start the stopwatch or clock.

3 Every minute check the films to see if they have cleared. When the gelatin has been digested by the protease the silver grains will fall away from the celluloid backing to leave a transparent film. Note down the time taken for each film to clear.

4 Draw a suitable graph or chart to display your results.

Sample results

Tube	Temperature in °C	Time to clear
1	10	6 mins 34 secs
2	20	3 mins 15 secs
3	30	2 mins 43 secs
4	40	3 mins 55 secs
5	50	8 mins 33 secs

Data response questions

1 Which tube cleared most rapidly?

2 Draw a graph to show the rate of enzyme activity at different temperatures.

3 What is the optimum temperature for this enzyme?

4 Why does the activity drop at higher temperatures?

5 How could you modify the experiment to get a more accurate estimate of the optimum temperature?

Answers are on page 125.

Discussion

The clearing of the film is a measure of enzyme activity: the faster the film clears the more active the enzyme. As expected the rate of enzyme activity rises with temperature. This is because the increase in temperature provides more energy for the chemicals to react together. However, above a certain temperature the heat begins to damage the three-dimensional shape of the protein molecule and this reduces its ability to breakdown protein. This is observed as a drop in enzyme activity at 50°C compared with 40°C.

QUESTIONS

Q1 What three chemical elements are present in all of the following: carbohydrates, proteins and fats?

Q2 How could you use ethanol and water to test for the presence of lipid in a sample of food? How does this test work?

Q3 Biological washing powders contain enzymes that can digest dirt at lower temperatures thus saving energy for heating water. Can you think of another reason for washing at lower temperatures when using a biological washing powder?

Answers are on page 158.

More questions
on the CD ROM

MOVEMENT OF SUBSTANCES INTO AND OUT OF CELLS

Videos & questions on the CD ROM

Organisms have to exchange materials with the environment. Food and oxygen has to get in, waste products need to get out. These materials need to pass through the cell membrane.

There are three main ways substances enter and leave cells:
1 diffusion
2 osmosis
3 active transport.

DIFFUSION

Substances like water, oxygen, carbon dioxide and food are made of particles (**molecules**).

In liquids and gases the particles are constantly moving around. This means that they will tend to spread themselves out evenly. For example, if you dissolve sugar in a cup of tea, even if you do not stir it, the sugar will eventually spread throughout the tea because the sugar molecules are constantly moving around, colliding with and bouncing off other particles. This is an example of **diffusion**.

> Diffusion is net movement of molecules from a region of high concentration to a region of low concentration.

- ● water molecule
- ● sugar molecule

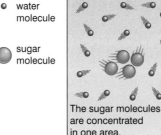

The sugar molecules are concentrated in one area.

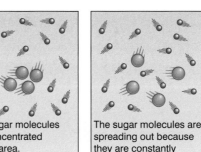

The sugar molecules are spreading out because they are constantly moving and colliding.

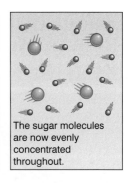

The sugar molecules are now evenly concentrated throughout.

Diffusion occurs when there is a **difference** in concentration. The greater the difference in concentration the faster the rate of diffusion.

Particles diffuse from regions of high concentration to regions of low concentration. They move down the **concentration gradient**.

Diffusion stops when the particles are evenly concentrated. But this does not mean that the particles themselves stop moving.

Diffusion happens because particles are constantly and randomly moving. It does not need an input of energy from a plant or animal.

Larger particles diffuse through membranes more slowly than smaller particles.

Diffusion in cells

Substances can enter and leave cells by diffusion. If there is a higher concentration on one side of the membrane than the other and the substance can move through the membrane, then it will.

For example, red blood cells travel to the lungs to collect oxygen. There is a **low** oxygen concentration in the red blood cells (because they have given up their oxygen to other parts of the body) and a **high** oxygen concentration in the alveoli of the lungs. Therefore oxygen diffuses into the red blood cells.

Other examples of diffusion include:

- carbon dioxide entering leaf cells

- digested food substances in the small intestine entering the blood

- in a kidney dialysis machine, the movement of urea from the dialysis tube into the dialysis fluid.

OSMOSIS

Osmosis is a special example of diffusion where **only water** molecules move into or out of cells. It occurs because cell membranes are **partially permeable**: they allow some substances (such as water) to move through them but not others. Usually, small molecules, such as water molecules, can pass through the membrane, but large molecules, such as sucrose sugar molecules, cannot.

Water molecules will diffuse from a place where there is a high concentration of water molecules (such as a dilute sucrose sugar solution) to where there is a low concentration of water molecules (such as a concentrated sucrose sugar solution).

Many people confuse the concentration of the solution with the concentration of the water. Remember, it is the **water molecules that are moving**, so you must think of the concentration of **water molecules in the solution** instead of the concentration of substance dissolved in it.

- A low concentration of dissolved substances means a high concentration of water molecules.

- A high concentration of dissolved substances means a low concentration of water molecules. So the water molecules are still moving from a **high concentration (of water molecules)** to a **low concentration (of water molecules)**, even though this is often described as water moving from a low-concentration solution to a high-concentration solution.

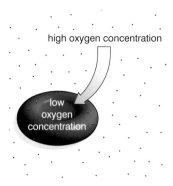

high oxygen concentration

low oxygen concentration

A high concentration gradient leads to a faster rate of diffusion. Red blood cells low in oxygen will absorb oxygen from oxygen-rich surroundings.

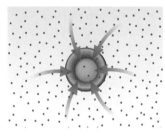

A red blood cell in pure water.

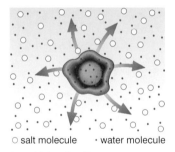

○ salt molecule   · water molecule

A red blood cell in a concentrated salt solution.

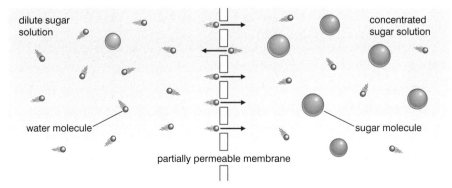

dilute sugar solution

concentrated sugar solution

water molecule

sugar molecule

partially permeable membrane

higher concentration of water molecules   lower concentration of water molecules

Water molecules diffuse from an area of higher concentration (of water molecules) into an area of lower concentration (of water molecules). This sort of diffusion is known as osmosis.

21

One important example of osmosis is water entering the roots of plants.

Water molecules enter a plant cell until the cytoplasm and vacuole push against the cell wall. The cell is then said to be **turgid**. Turgid cells are important for supporting the plant.

If a plant is losing water faster than it can absorb water from the soil, the plant cells will become **flaccid**. This is what is happening when a plant wilts.

If animal cells such as blood cells are placed in different strength solutions they will shrink or swell up (and even burst) depending on whether they gain or lose water molecules via osmosis.

Factors that increase the rate of diffusion or osmosis across cell membranes include a high surface area to volume ratio, a greater difference in concentration of a substance between the inside and outside of the cell (concentration gradient) and higher temperatures.

ACTIVE TRANSPORT

Sometimes cells need to absorb particles **against a concentration gradient**: from a region of low concentration into a region of high concentration.

For example, root hair cells may take in nitrate ions from the soil even though the concentration of these ions is higher in the plant than in the soil. The way that the nitrate ions are absorbed is called **active transport**. Another example of active transport is dissolved ions being actively absorbed back into the blood from kidney tubules.

Active transport occurs when special **carrier proteins** on the surface of a cell pick up particles from one side of the membrane and transport them to the other side. You can see this happening in the diagram below.

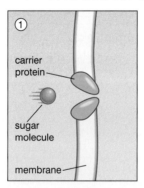 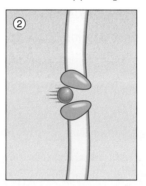 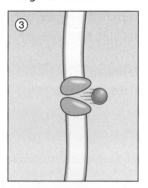

Active transport uses energy that the cells release during respiration.

The following experiments demonstrate osmosis and diffusion.

EXPERIMENT TO INVESTIGATE THE EFFECT OF SURFACE AREA TO VOLUME RATIO

This experiment looks at surface area to volume ratio as a factor in the speed at which materials can pass into the body.

You will need:
- Agar blocks – the easiest way to prepare these is in ice-cube trays to give individual blocks of approximately 4cm x 4cm x 3cm
- Modelling knife or scalpel
- 3 small dishes or beakers
- Dilute potassium (VII) manganate solution (0.1 mol dm^{-3}) (This is poisonous.)
- Cork borers (assorted sizes)
- Stopwatch
- Tweezers
- Hand lens

Measuring uptake:

1 Prepare a set of 5 agar cubes. They should all be 2cm x 2cm x 2cm.

2 Prepare a second set of 5 smaller agar cubes. Make this second set 1cm x 1cm x 1cm.

3 Prepare a third set of 5 agar cubes. These should be smaller again, aim for 0.5cm x 0.5cm x 0.5cm.

4 Place the set of large cubes in a dish or beaker and cover them completely with the potassium (VII) manganate solution. Start the stopwatch.

5 After 2 minutes take out one of the cubes and cut it in half. Estimate how far into the cube the potassium (VII) manganate colour has reached.

6 Repeat Step 5 four more times until all the cubes have been used and you have 5 figures for potassium (VII) mangate penetration.

7 Repeat the procedure using the second set of cubes.

8 Repeat the procedure using the third set of cubes.

Analysing the results:

1 Calculate the surface area for each of your cube sizes. The surface area of a cube is given by the formula:

Surface Area (SA) = 6 (length x width)

2 Calculate the volume for each of your cube sizes. The volume of a cube is given by the formula:

Volume (Vol) = length x width x height

Sample results

Cube length/width/height	2cm	1cm	0.5cm
Surface Area (SA)			
Volume (Vol)			
SA/Vol ratio			
Penetration of dye at 2 mins (%)	20	40	80
Penetration of dye at 4 mins (%)	40	80	100
Penetration of dye at 6 mins (%)	60	100	100
Penetration of dye at 8 mins (%)	80	100	100
Penetration of dye at 10 mins (%)	100	100	100

Data response questions

1 Which cube has the largest surface area to volume ratio?

2 What result would you expect if you used a 4cm cube?

3 Give reasons for your answer to question 2.

4 Cells lining the digestive system often have a frilly edge with a massively increased surface area. What is the advantage of this feature?

Answers are on page 125.

Discussion
The larger the surface area to volume ratio the more rapidly materials can pass into the body. Living organisms with large volumes make use of this phenomenon by having organs with extremely large surface areas (lungs or gills) to exchange gases with the environment.

EXPERIMENT TO MAKE A MODEL GUT

In this experiment a mixture of starch and enzyme is contained within a semi-permeable membrane. The enzyme breaks down the starch to smaller sugar molecules which can pass through the membrane of the tubing.

You will need:
- Deionised water
- Visking tubing (about 20cm in length)
- Amylase solution
- Starch solution
- Boiling tube
- Syringe
- Cotton or twine
- Beaker of deionised water warmed to 30°C
- Iodine solution
- Benedict's solution to test for sugar (or Clinistix)
- Stopwatch

Preparing the equipment:

1 Soak the Visking tubing in deionised water for a while. The tubing is supplied as a flat tape but when it has been soaked it can be opened up to produce a tube.

2 Mix 5ml of the amylase solution and 20ml of the starch solution in a boiling tube and then draw the mixture into the syringe.

3 Roll the open Visking tubing over the end of the syringe. Tie off the end with a knot and with cotton or twine. The knot must be waterproof.

4 Gently squeeze the contents of the syringe into the Visking tubing allowing the tubing to inflate like a balloon as you do this.

5 Remove the Visking tubing from the syringe and tie off the other end. You should now have a loosely-filled sausage of Visking tubing.

6 Carefully swill the Visking tubing sausage under the tap and then with deionised water. Now place it in a beaker of deionised water warmed to 30°C.

Collecting the results:
As you collect your results note them down in a table.

1 Test the starch solution, the amylase solution and the water in the beaker for starch using iodine solution.

2 Test the starch solution, the amylase solution and the water in the beaker for sugar using the Benedict's solution.

3 After 5 minutes test the water in the beaker for starch and sugar.

4 Repeat Step 3 every 5 minutes for the next 20 minutes.

Sample results

Time in minutes	Solution	Is starch present?	Is sugar present?
0	Starch	Yes	No
0	Amylase	No	No
0	Water in beaker	No	No
5	Water in beaker	No	No
10	Water in beaker	No	Yes
15	Water in beaker	No	Yes
20	Water in beaker	No	Yes

Data response questions

1 Why did you need to test the starch solution for the presence of sugar?

2 What do the results show about the permeability of Visking tubing to a) starch and b) sugar?

3 Amylase is a slow-acting enzyme and takes at least 10 minutes to produce sugar. Do your results support this statement?

Answers are on page 125.

Discussion

The initial tests show that none of the solutions contain sugar. The starch–amylase mixture is initially free of sugar as is the water surrounding it in the beaker. As the amylase breaks down the starch to sugar the smaller molecule can pass through the Visking tubing into the water in the beaker.

EXPERIMENT TO INVESTIGATE CHANGES IN WEIGHT DUE TO OSMOSIS

You will need:
- 5 boiling tubes and rack
- 25ml of 0.5M/l sodium chloride solution
- Distilled water
- Glass rod
- Paper towels
- Fresh root vegetables, e.g. potatoes
- Cork borer (at least size 12)
- Sharp knife
- Electronic balance capable of weighing to 0.001g
- 10ml measuring cylinder or syringe

Preparing the experimental solutions:

1 Label each boiling tube with a number from 1 to 5.

2 Pour 5ml of 0.5M/l sodium chloride solution into Tube 1.

3 Pour 5ml of 0.5M/l sodium chloride solution into Tube 2. Add 5ml of distilled water and stir with a dry glass rod. The solution in Tube 2 is now 0.25M/l.

4 Take 5ml of solution from Tube 2 and add to Tube 3. Add 5ml of distilled water to Tube 3 and stir with a dry glass rod. This makes a solution of 0.125M/l in Tube 3.

5 Take 5ml of solution from Tube 3 and place in Tube 4. Add 5ml of distilled water to Tube 4 and stir with a dry glass rod. Tube 4 now contains a solution of 0.0625M/l.

6 Pour 5ml of distilled water into Tube 5.

Preparing the discs:

1 Use the cork borer to prepare cores of fresh potato tissue.

2 Cut discs from these cores, each disc should be about 3mm deep.

3 Blot a collection of 5 discs dry with a paper towel. Weigh them with the electronic balance and note down the weight in a table.

4 Place the five discs in Tube 1.

5 Repeat the procedure above until you have 5 discs in each of the tubes. Leave the discs for at least two hours.

Collecting the results:

1 Remove the discs from Tube 1, blot them dry, weigh them and note down the weight in your table.

2 Repeat for all the tubes.

3 Calculate the change in weight of the discs in each tube and then the percentage change in weight. Plot a suitable graph or chart to display them.

Sample results

Tube	Weight at start/g	Weight at end/g	Weight change/g	Percentage change in weight
I	0.3I	0.237	-0.073	-30.8
2	0.273	0.290	+0.017	+5.86
3	0.290	0.325	+0.035	+10.77
4	0.325	0.375	+0.050	+13.33
5	0.320	0.376	+0.056	+17.5

Data response questions

1 Which set of disks showed the greatest percentage weight gain?

2 Draw a chart to show the percentage gain in each solution.

3 How can you explain the increase in weight in tubes 3, 4 and 5?

Answers are on page 125.

Discussion

Water passes into and out of the vegetable discs by osmosis. In salt solutions more dilute than the cell contents water tends to move in and so the discs gain weight. In more concentrated salt solutions more water passes out and so the discs lose weight. If there is no change in weight then the concentration of the cell contents must be the same as the concentration of the solution. Even if you do not have a tube in which there is no change in weight you should be able to estimate the concentration of the cell contents from drawing a graph. The concentration of the cell contents will be indicated by the point at which the line crosses the x-axis.

EXPERIMENT TO INVESTIGATE CHANGES IN SHAPE DUE TO OSMOSIS

Cells swell when they take in water. This experiment looks at changes in shape due to changes in cell inflation.

You will need:
• 3 boiling tubes
• Solution of sodium chloride 0.5M/l
• Distilled water
• Glass rod
• 5 Petri dishes
• Dandelion flower stalks – these must be fresh and kept in a beaker of water until needed
• Scalpel or modelling knife

Preparing the solutions:

1 Label each boiling tube with a number from 1 to 3.

2 Pour 5ml of 0.5M/l sodium chloride solution into Tube 1. Add 5ml of distilled water and stir.

Store the dandelion flower stalks in a beaker of water to keep them fresh.

3 Take 5ml of solution from Tube 1 and add to Tube 2. Add 5ml of distilled water to Tube 2 and stir.

4 Take 5ml of solution from Tube 2 and place in Tube 3. Add 5ml of distilled water to Tube 3 and stir.

Preparing the Petri dishes:
1 Label the Petri dishes from 1 to 5.

2 Add solutions to each Petri dish as shown in the table below.

Dish	Add	Concentration of solution in Petri dish
1	5ml of 0.5M/l sodium chloride solution	0.5M/l
2	Contents of Tube 1	0.25M/l
3	Contents of Tube 2	0.125M/l
4	Contents of Tube 3	0.0625M/l
5	5ml distilled water	zero

Preparing the dandelion samples:
1 Cut across the dandelion stalk to produce a cylinder roughly 5cm long.

2 Cut down the cylinder and unroll to produce a flat sheet.

3 Cut the flat sheet into strips. Keep them about 3mm wide along their whole length.

4 Add two strips to each Petri dish.

5 After about 5 minutes look at each of the strips to see if they have curled up. See if they have curled with the outer surface on the inside of the curl or on the outside. Note down your results. If they have not curled wait five more minutes and check the strips again.

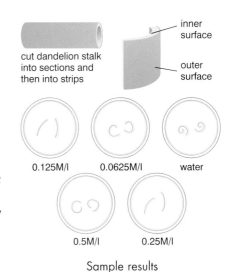

cut dandelion stalk into sections and then into strips

inner surface

outer surface

0.125M/l   0.0625M/l   water

0.5M/l   0.25M/l

Sample results

Data response questions

1 Which strips showed the greatest curvature?

2 Do all the strips curl the same way?

3 Explain how the curvature of the strips in the dish containing water was produced.

Answers are on page 125.

Discussion

In dilute solutions the dandelion strips curl up with the inner surface on the outside of the curl. In more concentrated solutions the strips curl with the inner surface on the inside of the curl. When water moves into a cell by osmosis the cell swells. In the dandelion stalk the outer surface is waterproofed with a waxy layer so water cannot enter or leave by osmosis and the cells cannot change size. When water enters cells on the inner surface they swell and push the stalk into a curl with the outer layer on the inside. For dandelion stalks in concentrated solutions water is drawn out of the cells and they shrink pulling the stalk into a curl with the inner cells on the inside of the curve. The solution that produces no curvature will have the same concentration as the cells.

Change in the shape of cells due to osmosis swelling can be useful to an organism, for example the opening and closing of guard cells in stomata.

EXPERIMENT TO INVESTIGATE PLASMOLYSIS CAUSED BY OSMOSIS

Cell membranes are not fixed to cell walls and so when they lose water by osmosis they draw away from each other to produce plasmolysed cells. This is easily observed in onion epidermal cells. By finding which concentration of solution produces only the smallest degree of plasmolysis, called incipient plasmolysis, it is possible to work out the concentration of the cell sap.

You will need:
- An onion
- Tweezers
- Scalpel
- Microscope slides and cover slips
- Microscope with low and high power lenses
- Paper towels
- Plain paper
- Sharp HB pencil
- Sucrose solution

1 Cut a section of onion and remove some of the very thin translucent sheet of epidermal cells with tweezers.

2 Cut a small square of the epidermal strip and place on a microscope slide in a drop of water. To place a cover slip gently on top, lay the cover slip down at one side just touching the water drop and then let the slip fall into place.

3 Look at the slide under low power on the microscope. Draw what you can see.

4 Repeat steps 1 to 3 with a fresh onion epidermal strip and use sucrose solution instead of water.

Cells mounted in water should be fully turgid with cell membranes pressed tightly against the cell walls. Cells mounted in concentrated sucrose solutions will show some plasmolysis with some cytoplasm separated from the cell walls. (If you use a red onion and select a sheet of cells from near the outside of the onion the cells are easier to see.)

QUESTIONS

Q1 An old-fashioned way of killing slugs in the garden is to sprinkle salt on them. This kills slugs by drying them out. Explain why this would dry them out.

Q2 Which of the following are examples of diffusion, osmosis or neither?
a Carbon dioxide entering a leaf when it is photosynthesising.
b Food entering your stomach when you swallow.
c Tears leaving your tear ducts when you cry.
d A dried out piece of celery swelling up when placed in a bowl of water.

Q3 Why would you expect plant root hair cells to respire faster than other plant cells?

Q4 Describe the difference between diffusion and active transport. Include one example of each in your answer.

More questions on the CD ROM

Answers are on pages 158–9.

NUTRITION

Nutrition in flowering plants

PHOTOSYNTHESIS

Plants need and use the same types of foods (carbohydrates, proteins and fats) as animals but, while animals have to eat other things to get their food, plants **make it themselves**. The way they do this is called **photosynthesis**. The other ways in which plants are different from animals, such as having leaves and roots, or being green, are all linked to photosynthesis.

In photosynthesis, plants take **carbon dioxide** from the air and **water** from the soil, and use the energy from **sunlight** to convert them into food. The first food they make is **glucose** but that can be changed later into other food types.

Oxygen is also produced in photosynthesis and, although some is used inside the plant for respiration (releasing energy from food), most is not needed and is given out as a **waste product** (although it is obviously vital for other living things).

The sunlight is absorbed by the green pigment **chlorophyll**.

The process of photosynthesis can be summarised in a **word equation**:

$$\text{carbon dioxide + water} \xrightarrow[\text{light}]{\text{chlorophyll}} \text{glucose + oxygen}$$

It can also be summarised as a balanced **symbol equation**:

$$6CO_2 + 6H_2O \xrightarrow[\text{light}]{\text{chlorophyll}} C_6H_{12}O_6 + 6O_2$$

Plants also require a number of inorganic ions which they absorb from the soil through their roots. These include nitrate ions which supply the nitrogen necessary for the formation of amino acids to build protein, and magnesium ions which are required for the manufacture of chlorophyll. A lack of either of these nutrients will cause yellowing of the green parts of plants.

Much of the glucose formed by photosynthesis is converted into other substances, such as **starch**. Starch molecules are made of lots of glucose molecules joined together. Starch is insoluble and so can be stored in the leaf without affecting water movement into and out of cells by **osmosis**.

Some glucose is converted to **sucrose** (a type of sugar consisting of two glucose molecules joined together), which is still soluble, but not as reactive as glucose, so can easily be carried around the plant in solution.

The energy needed to build up sugars into larger molecules comes from respiration.

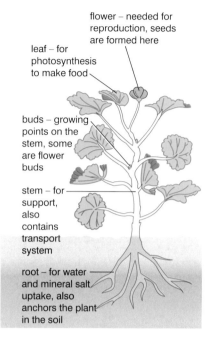

flower – needed for reproduction, seeds are formed here

leaf – for photosynthesis to make food

buds – growing points on the stem, some are flower buds

stem – for support, also contains transport system

root – for water and mineral salt uptake, also anchors the plant in the soil

Anatomy of a plant.

A* EXTRA

- For higher marks you will need to know the balanced chemical equation for photosynthesis.

The raw materials and products in a plant.

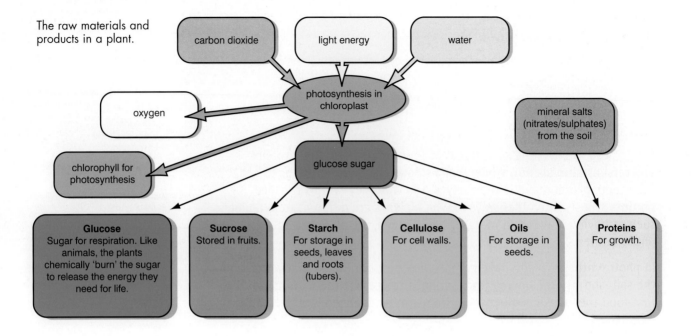

Where does photosynthesis occur?

Photosynthesis takes place mainly in the **leaves**, although it can occur in any cells that contain green chlorophyll. Leaves are adapted to make them very efficient as sites for photosynthesis.

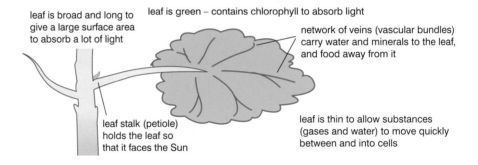

Leaves are **broad**, so as much light as possible can be absorbed.

Each leaf is **thin**, so it is easy for carbon dioxide to diffuse in to reach the cells in the centre of the leaf.

Leaves contain green **chlorophyll**, in the **chloroplasts**, which absorbs the light energy.

Leaves have **veins** to bring up water from the roots and carry food to other parts of the plant.

Each leaf has a stalk (**petiole**) that holds the leaf up at an angle so it can absorb as much light as possible.

Inside leaves

A leaf has a transparent **epidermis** to allow light to travel to the cells within the leaf.

There are many **palisade cells**, tightly packed together, in the uppermost half of the leaf, so that as many as possible can receive sunlight. Most photosynthesis takes place in these cells.

Chloroplasts containing chlorophyll are concentrated in cells in the uppermost half of the leaf to absorb as much sunlight as possible.

Air spaces in the spongy mesophyll layer allow the movement of gases (carbon dioxide and oxygen) through the leaf to and from cells.

A leaf has a large internal surface area to volume ratio to allow the efficient absorption of carbon dioxide and removal of oxygen by the photosynthesising cells.

Many pores or stomata (singular: stoma) allow the movement of gases into and out of the leaf.

Phloem tissue transports products of photosynthesis away from the leaf. Xylem tissue transports water and minerals to the leaf.

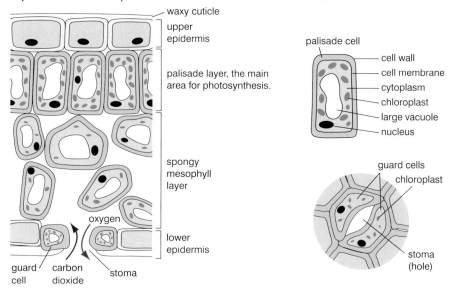

Cells of the leaf of a plant.

Limiting factors

If a plant gets more light, carbon dioxide or water or a higher temperature, then it might be able to photosynthesise at a faster rate. However, the rate of photosynthesis will eventually reach a maximum because there is not enough of one of the factors needed: one of them becomes a limiting factor.

For example, if a farmer pumps extra carbon dioxide into a greenhouse the rate of photosynthesis might increase so the crop will grow faster. But if the light is not bright enough to allow the plants to use the carbon dioxide as quickly as it is supplied, the light intensity would be the limiting factor. The graphs show how the rate of photosynthesis is affected by limiting factors.

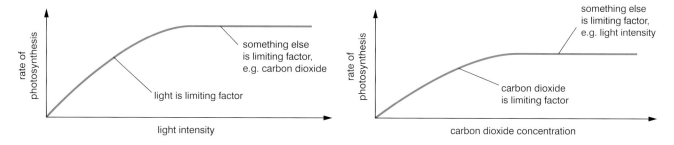

Increasing the levels of light and carbon dioxide, two of the factors necessary for photosynthesis, will increase the rate of photosynthesis until the rate is halted by some other limiting factor.

If the limiting factor in the first graph was the amount of carbon dioxide and the plants were then given more carbon dioxide, the graph would look like this:

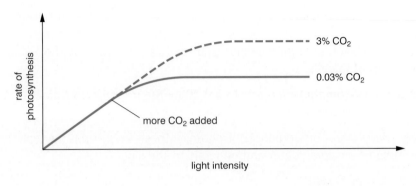

Temperature is also a limiting factor. Temperature affects the enzymes that control the rates of the chemical reactions of photosynthesis.

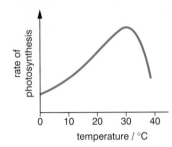

The following set of experiments looks at the conditions needed for photosynthesis.

EXPERIMENT TO INVESTIGATE THE REQUIREMENTS FOR LIGHT AND CARBON DIOXIDE

You will need:
- Pelargonium (Geranium) plant
- Ethanol
- White dish
- Iodine solution
- Aluminium foil
- Scissors
- Flask
- Sodium hydroxide or potassium hydroxide crystals

Before you can start the experiment you will need to destarch your geranium plant. This can be done by keeping it in a dark cupboard for a few days. The plant will use up the starch it has stored because it cannot produce any more by photosynthesis in the dark. To check that all starch stores have been depleted pluck off a leaf, plunge it into boiling water, wash in ethanol and then wash again in boiling water. This procedure kills the leaf and removes the outer surface of the leaf to allow the iodine solution you will add to reach the starch stores in the cells. Place the leaf on a white dish and add iodine solution. Any starch in the leaf will be stained dark blue-black.

Investigating light requirements:
Cut out a shape from aluminium foil. Fix this on a healthy leaf (still attached to the geranium) so that light can only pass onto the leaf through the cut-out shape. Leave the plant for two days in a lit area.

Investigating carbon dioxide requirements:
Fix a healthy stalk of the geranium in a flask containing sodium hydroxide or potassiuim hydroxide crystals, both of which readily absorb carbon dioxide. Do not let the leaf touch the crystals.

Remove the leaves that have been treated with the stencil or contained in the flask and test for starch as before.

Sample results
In the leaf with the stencil you should find that only the area that was exposed to light has starch. The leaf from the flask will not have any starch present. These experiments show that light and carbon dioxide are required for photosynthesis.

Data response questions

1 Why was the geranium plant destarched prior to the experiment?

2 Summarise the requirements for starch production in geraniums.

3 Why should you be careful when using sodium or potassium hydroxide?

Answers are on page 125.

EXPERIMENT TO INVESTIGATE CHLOROPHYLL AND PHOTOSYNTHESIS

Chlorophyll is a green pigment present in all photosynthetic plants. It is able to collect energy in sunlight and use this to drive the reactions that produce sugar and oxygen. For this experiment you will need a variegated plant (one with green and white patches on its leaves). A variegated geranium or a spider plant (*Chlorophytum comosum*) could be used. The plant should be destarched and tested as described above.

Once you have destarched your plant take it out of its cupboard and leave it for two days in a well lit area. Remove a leaf and test for starch. You will find that starch is only present in the green area of the leaf, the part containing chlorophyll. This shows that chlorophyll is required for photosynthesis.

EXPERIMENT TO INVESTIGATE LIGHT LEVELS AND PHOTOSYNTHESIS

Photosynthesis depends on light to drive the reaction. The level of light controls the rate of the reaction under certain conditions.

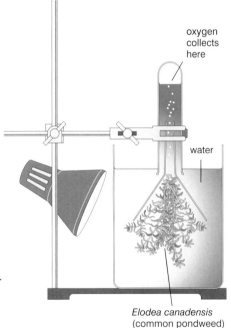

oxygen collects here

water

Elodea canadensis
(common pondweed)

You will need:
- Beaker of water
- Support stand and clamp
- Bench lamp
- Pondweed – *Elodea canadensis* (Canadian pondweed) is convenient to handle and easy to find. It is often sold for use in aquariums.
- Glass funnel
- Test tube
- Metre stick or tape measure
- Stopwatch or clock

1 Prepare a beaker of water next to a support stand and clamp. Position the bench lamp to shine onto the beaker. Put the pondweed into the wide end of the funnel and put the thin end of the funnel into a test tube that is full of water. Invert the funnel and test tube into the beaker of water, securing the test tube with the clamp. Record the distance between the lamp and the beaker containing the pondweed.

2 Count the number of bubbles of oxygen coming from the top of the pondweed over a 5-minute period.

3 Move the bench lamp closer to the pondweed and count the bubbles over the next 5 minutes.

4 Repeat until you have a range of values for distance from the pondweed to the light source.

Sample results

	Distance to lamp in cm				
	5	10	15	20	25
Oxygen bubbles given off in 5 minutes	67	57	40	20	4

Data response questions

1 Which distance gave the greatest rate of photosynthesis?

2 Draw a suitable graph or chart to show the relationship between light intensity (1/(distance from lamp to weed)^2) and photosynthesis (number of oxygen bubbles produced per unit time).

Answers are on page 125.

Discussion
Light intensity often acts as a limiting factor for photosynthesis so moving the light nearer to the pondweed will increase the rate of photosynthesis. However, results can be complicated by the carbon dioxide concentration. The pondweed might use up the carbon dioxide present in the water early on in the experiment and so reduce the rate of photosynthesis towards the end. The effect of this can be reduced by bubbling carbon dioxide gas through the water in between treatments with the light.

Nutrition in humans

A BALANCED DIET

To keep us healthy we need a **balanced diet**. A balanced diet needs to include:

Nuts are a valuable source of protein.

- **proteins** – which are broken down to make amino acids, which are themselves used to form enzymes and other proteins needed by cells. Protein sources include eggs, milk and milk products (cheese, yoghurt, etc.) meat, fish, legumes (peas and beans), nuts and seeds.

- **carbohydrates** – which are needed to release energy in our cells, to enable all the life processes to take place. Good sources of carbohydrate include rice, bread, potatoes, pasta and yams.

- **fat** – which is an important form of insulation to maintain body temperature, and is also used as a store of energy. Fat is present in meat and can also come in oils, milk products (butter, cheese), nuts, avocados and oily fish.

Vitamins and minerals	Job	Good food source	Deficiency disease
Vitamin A	Helps cells to grow and keeps skin healthy, helps eyes to see in poor light	Liver, vegetables, butter, fish oil and milk	**Night blindness**
Vitamin B	For healthy skin and to keep the nervous system working properly	Meat, eggs, vegetables, fish and milk	**Beri-beri** (leg muscles are unable to grow properly)
Vitamin C	For healthy skin, teeth and gums, and keeps lining of blood vessels healthy	Citrus fruit and green vegetables	**Scurvy** (bleeding gums and wounds do not heal properly)
Vitamin D	For strong bones and teeth	Fish, eggs, liver, cheese and milk	**Rickets** (softening of the bones)
Calcium	Needed for strong teeth and bones, and involved in the clotting of blood	Milk and eggs	**Rickets** (softening of the bones)
Iron	Needed to make haemoglobin in red blood cells	Meat and spinach	**Anaemia** (reduction in number of red blood cells, person soon becomes tired and short of breath)

- **vitamins** and **minerals** – which are needed for the correct functioning of the body. Vitamins and minerals cannot be produced by the body and cooking food destroys some vitamins. This is why it is so important to eat raw fruit and vegetables.

- **fibre** – which is made up of the cell walls of plants. It adds bulk to food so that it can be easily moved along the digestive system by peristalsis. This is important in preventing constipation. Fibre is thought to help prevent bowel cancer.

- **water** – which is the major constituent of the body of living organisms and is necessary for all life processes. Water is continually being lost through excretion and must be replaced regularly in order to maintain health.

Too much **saturated fat** (animal fat) causes **cholesterol** to be deposited inside blood vessels, making them narrower (as shown in the diagram left). The heart needs to work harder trying to push blood through these narrow vessels. This increases the risk of heart attack.

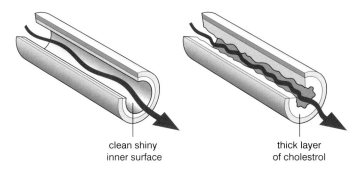

clean shiny
inner surface

thick layer
of cholestrol

It is important to match your diet with:
- how active you are
- your age and gender
- your body size.

	Energy used in a day (kJ)	
	Male	**Female**
6-year-old child	7500	7500
12–15-year-old teenager	12 500	9700
Adult manual worker	15 000	12 500
Adult office worker	11 000	9800
Pregnant woman		10 000

DIGESTION

If the food we eat is to be of any use to us it must enter our blood so that it can **travel to every part of the body**.

Many of the foods we eat are made up of **large, insoluble molecules** that would not easily enter the blood. This means they have to be **broken down into small, soluble molecules** that can easily enter and be carried dissolved in the blood. Breaking down the molecules is called **digestion**.

There are two stages of digestion.

1 **Physical digestion** occurs mainly in the mouth, where food is broken down into smaller pieces by the teeth and tongue.

2 **Chemical digestion** is the breakdown of large food molecules into smaller ones.

Some molecules, such as glucose, vitamins, minerals and water, are already small enough to pass through the gut wall and do not need to be digested.

Breaking down food for absorption by chemical digestion. The names of specific enzymes are shown above and below the blue arrows.

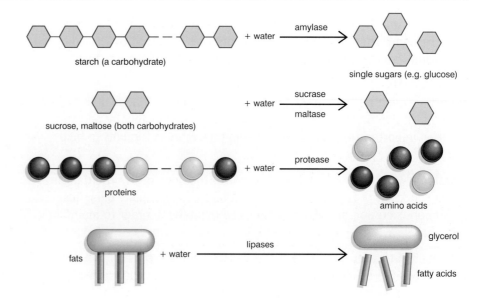

Chemical digestion happens because of chemicals called **enzymes**. Enzymes are a type of **catalyst** found in living things.

Every cell contains many enzymes, which control the many chemical reactions that happen inside it. **Digestive enzymes** are only one type of enzyme. They are produced in the cells lining parts of the digestive system and are **secreted** (produced) to mix with the food.

There are different **groups** of digestive enzymes, such as:

- **proteases** (produced by the stomach wall) – which break down proteins to amino acids

- **lipases** (produced by the pancreas) – which break down fats to fatty acids and glycerol

- **amylase** (produced by the salivary glands) – which breaks down starch into single sugars, e.g glucose and disaccharides, e.g maltose

- **maltase**, **sucrase** and **lactase** (produced by the small intestine) – which break down the sugars maltose, sucrose and lactose.

SUBSTANCES THAT HELP DIGESTION

Hydrochloric acid is secreted in the stomach. This is important to **kill bacteria** in food. Also, the enzymes in the stomach work best at a **low (acidic) pH.**

Sodium hydrogencarbonate is secreted from the pancreas to **neutralise the acid** leaving the stomach so that the enzymes in the small intestine can work.

Bile is produced in the liver, stored in the gall bladder, and passes along the bile duct into the duodenum. Bile **emulsifies fats**. It breaks down large fat droplets

Bile lowers the surface tension of large droplets of fat so that they break up. This part of the digestive process is called emulsification.

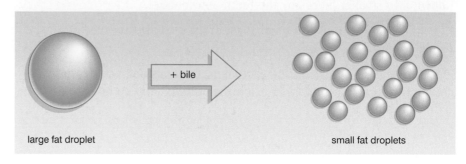

large fat droplet   small fat droplets

into smaller ones, which means that a larger surface area is exposed for chemical reactions to take place. It also contains **bicarbonate ions** to help neutralise **stomach acids.**

THE DIGESTIVE SYSTEM

Eating food involves several different processes:
- **ingestion** – taking food into the body
- **digestion** of food into small molecules
- **absorption** of digested food into the blood
- **egestion** – removal of indigestible material (**faeces**) from the body.

Remember that egestion is not the same as **excretion**, which is the removal of waste substances that have been made in the body.

All these different processes take place in different parts of the **digestive system** (the **alimentary canal**).

Food moves along the digestive system because of the **contractions** of the muscles in the walls of the alimentary canal. This is called **peristalsis.**

Peristalsis moves food along the digestive system.

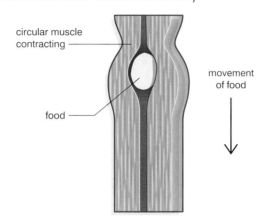

circular muscle contracting

food

movement of food

muscular wall of gullet

Part of digestive system	What happens there
Mouth	Teeth and tongue break down food into smaller pieces Saliva from salivary glands moistens food so it is easily swallowed and contains amylase to begin breakdown of starch
Oesophagus or gullet	Each lump of swallowed food, called a **bolus**, is moved along by waves of muscle contraction called **peristalsis**
Stomach	Food enters through a ring of muscle known as a **sphincter** Acid and protease are secreted to start protein digestion Movements of the muscular wall churn up food into a liquid known as **chyme** (pronounced 'kime') The bulk of the food is stored while the partly digested food passes a little at a time through another sphincter into the duodenum
Gall bladder	Stores bile. The bile is passed along the bile duct into the duodenum
Pancreas	Secretes amylase, lipase and protease as well as sodium hydrogencarbonate into the duodenum
Small intestine (made up of duodenum and ileum)	Secretions from the gall bladder and pancreas as well as sucrase, maltase, lactase, protease and lipase from the wall of the duodenum complete digestion Digested food is absorbed into the blood through the villi
Large intestine or colon	Water is absorbed from the remaining material
Rectum	The remaining material (**faeces**), made up of indigestible food, dead cells from the lining of the alimentary canal and bacteria, is compacted and stored
Anus	Faeces is egested through a sphincter
Liver	Cells in the liver make bile. Amino acids not used for making proteins are converted into glycogen in the liver. Millions of red blood cells are broken down every day, and iron from their haemoglobin is stored in the liver. Vitamins A and D are stored in the liver. Poisonous compounds that are either produced by the body or enter the body are converted in to harmless substances. The liver removes excess glucose from the blood and stores it as glycogen.

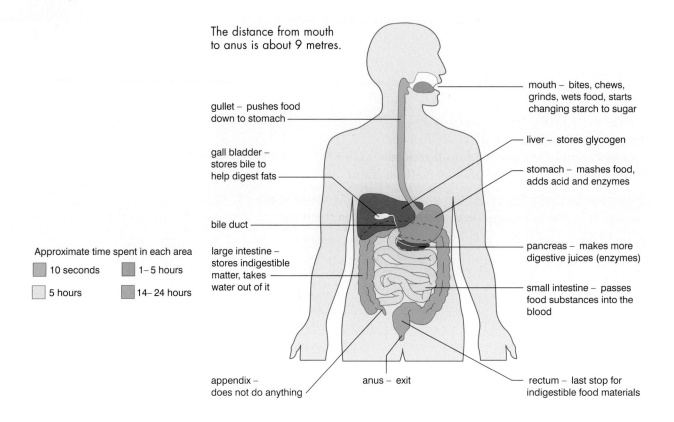

The distance from mouth to anus is about 9 metres.

mouth – bites, chews, grinds, wets food, starts changing starch to sugar

gullet – pushes food down to stomach

liver – stores glycogen

gall bladder – stores bile to help digest fats

stomach – mashes food, adds acid and enzymes

bile duct

Approximate time spent in each area

10 seconds   1–5 hours

5 hours   14–24 hours

large intestine – stores indigestible matter, takes water out of it

pancreas – makes more digestive juices (enzymes)

small intestine – passes food substances into the blood

appendix – does not do anything

anus – exit

rectum – last stop for indigestible food materials

ABSORPTION OF FOOD

After food has been digested it can enter the blood. This happens in the main part of the small intestine, known as the **ileum**. To help this process, the lining of the ileum is covered in millions of small finger-like projections called **villi** (singular: villus).

The ileum is adapted for efficient absorption of food by having a large surface area. This is because:

- it is **long** (6–7 metres in an adult)

- the inside is covered with **villi**

- the villi are covered in **microvilli**.

The structure of the ileum.

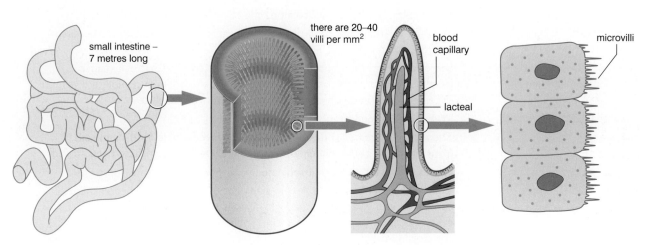

small intestine – 7 metres long

there are 20–40 villi per mm²

blood capillary

microvilli

lacteal

The villi themselves have features that also help absorption:

- they have **thin, permeable walls**

- they have a **good blood supply**, which maintains a concentration gradient that aids diffusion

- they contain **lymph vessels** (lacteals), which absorb some of the fat.

The lymph vessels eventually drain into the blood system.

ASSIMILATION

Assimilation is the name for the processes by which food that has been digested and absorbed from the intestines is then utilised in the body.

Most of the nutrients absorbed from the small intestine pass straight to the liver by means of the hepatic portal vein. Vitamins A, B and D and iron, are stored in liver cells. If there is enough glucose in the blood, insulin from the pancreas stimulates liver cells to take up surplus glucose and store it as glycogen. When blood sugar levels fall below a critical level, another hormone stimulates the liver cells to release glucose back into the blood. If the glucose stores are full, any extra glucose is converted into fat in special fat-storage cells round the body. Regulating blood glucose concentration is an example of homeostasis.

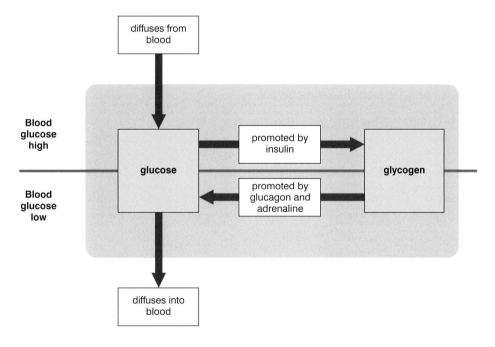

Regulation of blood glucose.

Active cells need amino acids to build proteins, but when more are absorbed than are needed, the surplus amino acids cannot be stored. Some kinds of amino acids can be converted into other kinds that are needed. The rest are broken down in the liver and parts of the molecule are recycled. This is called deamination. The main part of the molecule is converted into glucose or other compounds, but the 'amino' part has to be excreted, because its breakdown product is alkaline and would disturb the pH balance of body fluids. It is converted into a less harmful form called urea. This chemical is carried in the blood to the kidneys, and excreted in urine.

EXPERIMENT TO EXAMINE THE ENERGY CONTENT OF A FOOD SAMPLE

The energy contained within plants forms the basis for all life in an area and, where the joule value is high, the animal life in the area is also abundant. However, this assumes that the animals can extract the energy from the plants by digestion. Wood, for example, has a high joule value but is very difficult to break down.

You will need:

- 100ml Pyrex™ beaker
- Clamp and support stand
- Thermometer (–10 to 110°C)
- Samples of dried plant material, e.g., a woody twig, grass, a waxy leaf like holly, an almond or a brazil nut, or other oily seed, etc.
- Electric balance
- 50ml graduated cylinder
- Tongs
- Bunsen burner
- Calculator

1 Secure the beaker in the clamp. Position the beaker at a height that will allow you to hold the plant material in tongs below the beaker. Also secure a thermometer in the beaker. Ensure that the beaker is held firmly in the clamp, but do not over tighten its jaws and crack the glass.

2 Weigh the sample of plant material you plan to burn. Aim for a sample weighing between 10 and 25 grams.

3 Pour 25ml of water into the beaker and record the temperature of the water in a table like the one below.

4 Hold the sample of plant material in the tongs and light it with the Bunsen burner. As soon as it catches fire, transfer it to a position immediately underneath the beaker of water so that as much of the heat as possible goes into the water.

5 If the plant material stops burning, light it again quickly with the Bunsen burner and then return it to its position below the beaker.

6 When the plant material will no longer burn, quickly take the temperature of the water in the beaker and record this value in the data table.

7 Repeat Steps 2–6 with other samples of dried plant material and fresh cold water.

8 Calculate the energy released by the sample. Remember that 4.2 joules is the amount of energy required to raise 1g (1cm^3) of water through 1°C.

Sample results

	Plant sample		
	Nut	Wood	Leaf
Mass of sample in grams	22	25	12
Temperature of water after burning in °C	27	22	16
Temperature of water before burning in °C	15	15	15
Temperature rise in °C	12	7	1
Energy released by the sample in joules	1260	735	105

Data response questions

1 Which sample produced the lowest increase in temperature?

2 Why did you need to calculate the energy release per gram of material and not simply the energy released?

3 How could you explain the difference in energy release per gram between the leaf and the nut?

Answers are on page 125.

Discussion

Seeds have the best combination of high joule value and accessibility; they are adapted to be energy stores for the growing plants. This explains why so much of our food is based on seeds rather than the much more common vegetative parts of a plant.

Inaccuracies in the experiment will come from heat being wasted and not passing into the water. This will lead to a lower temperature rise in the water and an under-estimate of the energy value of the sample material. Similarly incomplete combustion of the sample will produce an underestimate.

QUESTIONS

Q1 **a** How does a plant get the raw materials it needs for photosynthesis?
b Why are leaves usually broad and thin?

Q2 **a** Protein molecules are long chains of amino acid molecules joined together. Why do proteins need to be digested?
b What is the difference between physical and chemical digestion?
c What happens to enzymes at high temperatures?
d Why is alkaline sodium hydrogencarbonate secreted into the duodenum?

Q3 **a** What is the difference between ingestion, egestion and excretion?
b Where do ingestion and egestion happen?

More questions
on the CD ROM

Answers are on page 159.

RESPIRATION

Videos & questions
on the CD ROM

The energy that our bodies need to keep us alive is released from our food.
Releasing the energy is called **respiration** and happens in every cell of our
body. The food is usually **glucose** (sugar) but other kinds of food can be
used if there is not enough glucose available.

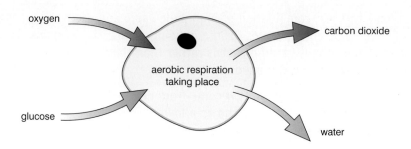

Different foods contain different amounts of **energy**. Carbohydrates (such as
glucose) and proteins contain a similar amount of energy, but fat contains
nearly twice the amount of energy.

The amount of energy in food is measured using a **calorimeter**. The amount
of energy used to be measured in calories, but now it is measured in **joules**.

Respiration usually involves **oxygen**. This kind of respiration is called **aerobic
respiration**. Water and carbon dioxide are produced as waste products. This
is very similar to burning fuel. However, in our bodies enzymes control the
rate at which energy is released.

Aerobic respiration can be summarised by a word equation:

glucose + oxygen → water + carbon dioxide + energy

It can also be written as a symbol equation:

$$C_6H_{12}O_6 + 6O_2 \rightarrow 6H_2O + 6CO_2 + 2900 \text{ kJ}$$

The important number to remember is **6**.

The energy released is used for all the other processes of life: movement,
sensitivity, growth, reproduction, excretion and nutrition (feeding).
Eventually most of the energy is lost as heat.

Aerobic respiration provides most of the energy we need. During exercise
we need more energy so the rate of aerobic respiration increases:

- muscle cells need more glucose and oxygen

- more glucose is removed from the blood

- breathing becomes faster and deeper, to take in more oxygen

- the heart rate increases to deliver the oxygen and glucose to the muscle
  cells more quickly.

ANAEROBIC RESPIRATION

There is a limit to how fast we can breathe and how fast the heart can beat. This means that the muscles might not get enough oxygen. In this case another kind of respiration is used that does not need oxygen. This is called **anaerobic respiration.**

Anaerobic respiration in human cells can be summarised by a word equation:

glucose $\rightarrow$ lactic acid + energy

Anaerobic respiration can also occur in plants but here glucose is converted to ethanol, carbon dioxide and energy. This is known as fermentation.

The word equation for fermentation is:

glucose $\rightarrow$ ethanol + carbon dioxide + energy

The symbol equation is:

$$C_6H_{12}O_6 \rightarrow 2C_2H_5OH + 2CO_2$$

Anaerobic respiration, whether in plants or animals, releases much less energy than aerobic respiration.

Differences between aerobic and anaerobic respiration	
Aerobic respiration	**Anaerobic respiration**
Uses oxygen	Does not use oxygen
Releases a large amount of energy	Releases a small amount of energy
Does not make lactic acid or ethanol	Makes lactic acid or ethanol
Makes carbon dioxide	Does not always make carbon dioxide
Makes water	Does not make water

THE OXYGEN DEBT

The **lactic acid** that builds up during anaerobic respiration is poisonous. It causes muscle fatigue (tiredness) and makes muscles ache.

Lactic acid has to be broken down, and oxygen is needed to do this. This is why you continue to breathe quickly even after you have finished exercising. You are taking in the extra oxygen you need to remove the lactic acid. This is sometimes called **repaying the oxygen debt.**

Only when all the lactic acid has been broken down do your heart rate and breathing return to normal.

At the end of a race, athletes can be in a lot of pain because of the lactic acid released by anaerobic respiration in the muscle cells.

EXPERIMENT TO SHOW THE PRODUCTION OF CARBON DIOXIDE AND HEAT BY LIVING ORGANISMS

All living things carry out respiration continuously to provide energy for their cellular reactions. This produces carbon dioxide and heat as by-products.

You will need:
- Disinfectant and deionised water
- Pea or bean seeds
- 2 Thermos flasks fitted with bung and glass tubes
- 2 thermometers (-10°C to 110°C)
- Limewater (or hydrogen carbonate indicator) solution
- 2 sets of delivery tubing
- 2 boiling tubes and rack

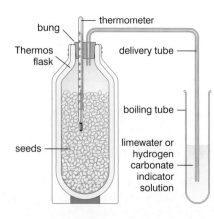

bung — thermometer
Thermos flask — delivery tube
boiling tube
seeds
limewater or hydrogen carbonate indicator solution

1 Soak the seeds for a day. This will help them to germinate. Sterilise the surface of the seeds by gently washing in a suitable disinfectant and then swill off in deionised water. This kills any microorganisms present on the seed surface that might produce carbon dioxide and confuse the results.

2 Pack the seeds into the Thermos flask and position a thermometer through the bung of the flask. Connect delivery tubing from the glass tube in the flask across to a boiling tube of limewater or hydrogen carbonate indicator solution. The boiling tube should stand in a rack.

3 Assemble an identical experiment without the seeds.

4 Make observations of the liquid in the boiling tubes daily for about 5 days.

Sample results

		Seeds in Thermos	No seeds in Thermos
Start	Observation	Clear	Clear
	Temperature in °C	15	15
After 1 day	Observation		
	Temperature in °C		
After 2 days	Observation	Milky	Clear
	Temperature in °C	19	15

Data response questions

1 Which gas is detected by limewater?

2 How can you tell that the seeds produced the change in the limewater?

3 Why were the seeds packed in a Thermos flask?

Answers are on page 125.

Discussion
The limewater in the boiling tube connected to the Thermos flask with seeds goes milky to show the presence of carbon dioxide. (Hydrogen carbonate indicator would turn from orangey-red to yellow to show the same effect.) The liquid in the tube connected to the Thermos without seeds is unchanged. Seeds produce carbon dioxide and heat by respiration. The Thermos without seeds is required as a control.

Similar experiments can be performed with maggots or woodlice although the change in the limewater would be faster and air would have to be continually drawn through the equipment to ensure the animals had sufficient oxygen.

QUESTIONS

Q1 Why do living things respire?

Q2 Where does respiration happen?

Q3 a Why is aerobic respiration better than anaerobic respiration?
   b If aerobic respiration is better, why does anaerobic respiration sometimes happen?

Answers are on page 159.

More questions on the CD ROM

GAS EXCHANGE

Diffusion

Gas exchange in both plants and humans depends upon the process of diffusion. In plants gases enter and leave the leaf by means of diffusion through the stomata. In humans gases drawn into the lungs diffuse across the thin walls of the alveoli and into the blood. In both plants and animals gases enter and leave the cells by diffusion.

Gas exchange in flowering plants

PHOTOSYNTHESIS AND RESPIRATION

Once plants have made food using sunlight, they will at some stage need to release the energy in the food. They do this in the same way that humans and other animals do: **respiration**.

During the day, plants respire 'slower' than they photosynthesise, so we only detect carbon dioxide entering and oxygen leaving the plant. During the night, photosynthesis stops and then we can detect oxygen entering and carbon dioxide leaving during respiration.

At dawn and dusk, the rates of photosynthesis and respiration are the same and **no gases enter or leave** the plant because any oxygen produced by photosynthesis is immediately used up in respiration, and any carbon dioxide produced is used up in photosynthesis. These occasions are known as **compensation points**.

We have already considered the structure of the leaf when looking at photosynthesis (page 29). Carbon dioxide and oxygen enter and leave the plant through the stomata. Normally the stomata open wider when the leaf is exposed to light and tend to close again during the dark. This is because there is a greater demand for gas exchange while the plant is photosynthesising as well as respiring. This opening and closing is controlled by changes in the shape of the guard cells surrounding the stomata. When they swell the change in shape opens the stomata. When the cells lose turgor, the cells return to their original shape and the stomata close.

Within the leaf the air spaces in the spongy mesophyll allow gases to diffuse to all the cells – the leaf has a large internal surface area. Because leaves are thin gases never have far to travel.

EXPERIMENT TO INVESTIGATE LIGHT LEVELS AND NET GAS EXCHANGE IN LEAF DISCS

Leaves carry out photosynthesis during the daylight and respiration at all times. In daylight, photosynthesis occurs more rapidly than respiration so the level of carbon dioxide near a leaf falls. This can be detected by a change in the colour of hydrogen carbonate indicator. As the light level falls the rate of photosynthesis falls so the level of carbon dioxide rises.

Videos & questions on the CD ROM

Because leaves are thin, gases never have far to travel.

You will need:
- Hydrogen carbonate indicator solution
- Flask
- Pump
- Fresh healthy leaves (cabbage or spinach are suitable)
- Core borers (1cm or larger diameter)
- 2 Petri dishes
- Syringe
- Lamp or other source of light
- Black paper

Preparing the hydrogen carbonate solution:

1 Place the hydrogen carbonate indicator solution in a flask and draw air through the solution with a pump. This will ensure that the carbon dioxide concentration in the solution will match that of the atmosphere. It should take less than 10 minutes and the solution will look red-orange when it is complete. The solution is now known as equilibrated hydrogen carbonate indicator solution.

Monitoring the carbon dioxide exchange:

1 Wash the leaves and cut 20 discs, avoiding midribs and large veins.

2 Divide the discs equally between two Petri dishes. Using the syringe, add 10ml of equilibrated hydrogen carbonate indicator solution to each dish and note the colour.

3 Place the dishes on a windowsill or in a well-illuminated position. Note the colour of the indicator solution in both dishes and then cover one of them with black paper to block out all light.

4 Note the colour of the indicator in both dishes every 2 minutes for the next 10 minutes. Keep the 'dark dish' exposed to the light for the smallest possible time.

When cutting the discs from the leaves avoid the midribs and large veins.

Sample results

Time in minutes	Light dish	Dark dish
0	Red-orange	Red-orange
2	Red	Light orange
4	Reddish-purple	Yellowish-orange
6	Purple	Yellow
8	Purple	Yellow
10	Purple	Yellow

Data response questions

1 What does hydrogen carbonate indicator react to?

2 What caused the change in indicator colour in the light dish?

3 What caused the colour change in the dark dish?

Answers are on page 125.

Discussion

A plant carries out respiration at all times and photosynthesis in the light. In well-lit conditions the rate of photosynthesis is much higher than the rate of respiration so carbon dioxide is taken in and oxygen is released. This means the hydrogen carbonate indicator becomes more alkaline and turns purple in colour. In the dark photosynthesis stops so no carbon dioxide is taken in. Respiration continues and produces carbon dioxide. This dissolves in the hydrogen carbonate solution reducing its pH and turning it yellow.

Gas exchange in humans

BREATHING IS NOT RESPIRATION

Breathing is the way that oxygen is taken into our bodies and carbon dioxide removed. Sometimes it is called **ventilation**.

Do not confuse breathing with respiration. Respiration is a chemical process that happens in every cell in the body. Unfortunately, the confusion is not helped when you realise that the parts of the body responsible for breathing are known as the **respiratory system**.

HOW WE BREATHE

When we breathe, air is moved into and out of our lungs. This involves different parts of the respiratory system inside the **thorax** (chest cavity).

When we **breathe in**, air enters though the nose and mouth. In the nose the air is moistened and warmed.

The air travels down the **trachea** (windpipe) to the lungs. Tiny hairs called **cilia** help to remove dirt and microbes.

The air enters the lungs through the **bronchi** (singular: bronchus), which branch and divide to form a network of **bronchioles**.

At the end of the bronchioles are air sacs. The bulges on an air sac are called **alveoli** (singular: alveolus). The alveoli are covered in tiny blood capillaries. This is where oxygen enters the blood and carbon dioxide leaves the blood.

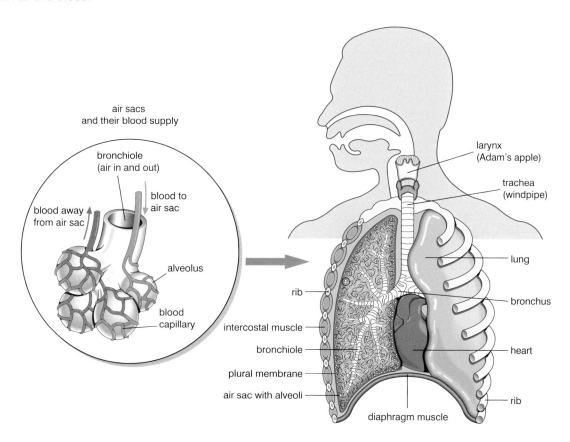

air sacs
and their blood supply

bronchiole
(air in and out)

blood to
air sac

blood away
from air sac

alveolus

blood
capillary

larynx
(Adam's apple)

trachea
(windpipe)

lung

rib

bronchus

intercostal muscle

bronchiole

heart

plural membrane

air sac with alveoli

rib

diaphragm muscle

INHALATION AND EXHALATION

Breathing in is known as **inhalation** and breathing out as **exhalation** (sometimes they are called inspiration and expiration).

Both happen because of changes in the volume of the thorax. The change in volume causes pressure changes, which in turn cause air to enter or leave the lungs.

The changes in thorax volume are caused by the **diaphragm**, which is a domed sheet of muscle under the lungs, and the **intercostal muscles**, which connect the ribs. There are two sets of intercostals: the internal intercostal muscles and the external intercostal muscles.

Inhalation
Air is breathed into the lungs as follows.

1 The diaphragm **contracts** and **flattens** in shape.

2 The external intercostal muscles **contract**, making the ribs move upwards and outwards.

3 These changes cause the **volume** of the thorax to **increase**.

4 This causes the **air pressure** inside the thorax to **decrease**.

5 This causes air to **enter** the lungs.

Rings of **cartilage** in the trachea, bronchi and bronchioles keep the air passages open and prevent them from collapsing when the air pressure decreases.

A* EXTRA

- During inhalation air enters because the air pressure inside the lungs is lower than the air pressure outside the body.
- During exhalation air leaves the lungs because the air pressure inside is higher than the air pressure outside the body.

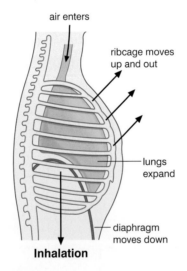

air enters

ribcage moves up and out

lungs expand

diaphragm moves down

Inhalation

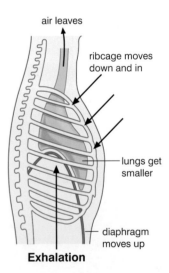

air leaves

ribcage moves down and in

lungs get smaller

diaphragm moves up

Exhalation

Exhalation
Air is breathed out from the lungs as follows.

1 The diaphragm **relaxes** and returns to its **domed** shape, pushed up by the liver and stomach. This means **it pushes up on the lungs**.

2 The external intercostal muscles **relax**, allowing the ribs to drop back down. This also presses on the lungs. If you are breathing hard the internal intercostal muscles also contract, helping the ribs to move down.

3 These changes cause the **volume** of the thorax to **decrease**.

4 This causes the **air pressure** inside the thorax to **increase**.

5 This causes air to **leave** the lungs.

COMPOSITION OF INHALED AND EXHALED AIR

The air we breathe in and out contains many gases. **Oxygen** is taken into the blood from the air we breathe in. **Carbon dioxide** and **water vapour** are added to the air we breathe out. The other gases in the air we breathe in are breathed out almost unchanged, except for being warmer.

	In inhaled air	In exhaled air
Oxygen	21%	16%
Carbon dioxide	0.04%	4.5%
Nitrogen and other gases	79%	79%
Water	Variable	High
Temperature	Variable	High

ALVEOLI

The **alveoli** are where oxygen and carbon dioxide diffuse into and out of the blood. For this reason the alveoli are described as the site of **gaseous exchange** or the **respiratory surface**.

The alveoli are **adapted** (have special features) to make them efficient at gaseous exchange. They have:

• **thin, permeable walls** – to allow a short pathway for diffusion

• a **moist lining** – in which oxygen dissolves first before it diffuses through

• a **large surface area** – there are lots of alveoli, providing a very large surface area

• a **good supply of oxygen** and **good blood supply** – which means that a concentration gradient is maintained so oxygen and carbon dioxide can rapidly diffuse across.

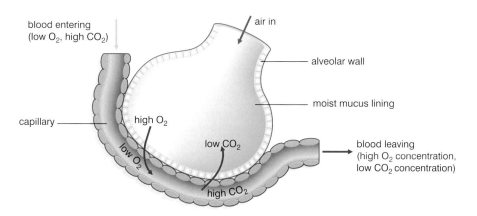

Gaseous exchange in an air-filled alveolus.

Tobacco smoke contains both tar and carbon monoxide.

SMOKING

Tobacco contains **nicotine**, which is a stimulant that increases blood pressure and is addictive. Nicotine can also lead to the formation of blood clots, increasing the chances of heart disease.

Tobacco smoke contains **tar**, which irritates the lining of the air passages in the lungs, making them inflamed and causing **bronchitis**. Tar can cause the lining cells to multiply, leading to **lung cancer**. Tar also damages the cilia lining the air passages and causes **extra mucus** to be made, which trickles down into the lungs because the cilia can no longer remove it. Bacteria can breed in the mucus so you are more likely to get chest infections and **smokers' cough** as your body tries to get rid of the mucus. The **alveoli** are also damaged, so it is more difficult to absorb oxygen into the blood. This condition is known as **emphysema**.

Tobacco smoke contains **carbon monoxide**, which stops red blood cells from carrying oxygen by combining irreversibly with the haemoglobin in the cells. This could also seriously affect the development of the fetus in the womb of a pregnant smoker, leading to a baby with low birth weight.

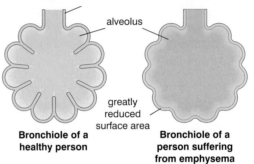

alveolus

greatly reduced surface area

Bronchiole of a healthy person

Bronchiole of a person suffering from emphysema

EXPERIMENT TO INVESTIGATE EXERCISE, BREATHING AND PULSE RATES

Muscles require a constant supply of energy and this is provided by respiration. Respiration in turn requires food and oxygen, both of which are supplied by the blood. Any increase in activity should show a corresponding increase in the rate of blood flow (measured by pulse rate) and oxygen intake (measured by breathing rate).

You will need:
- Large plastic bottle (about 2l)
- Indelible marker
- Water trough
- Plastic tubing with mouthpiece and nose clip
- Antiseptic solution
- Stopwatch
- Bench or step

1 In order to calibrate the plastic bottle, pour a measured amount of water (500ml) at a time) into the bottle and mark the level on the side of the bottle with the indelible marker. Repeat this process until the bottle is full and then invert the bottle into the water trough without allowing any air into the bottle. Introduce the plastic tubing into the bottle and secure both the bottle and the tubing in position. Use the antiseptic solution to clean the mouthpiece on the tubing.

2 Allow the experimental subject to rest and then take their breathing rate. The easiest way to do this is to count the number of breaths per minute. Monitor their breathing over 5 minutes to get a valid result. Also note down the pulse rate by counting the beats detected at the wrist or neck in 20 seconds and multiplying by 3 to give a beats per minute value.

3 During this rest period you should also measure the volume of air per breath. To do this, ask the subject to wear the nose clip and breathe out through the mouthpiece into the tubing. You can then measure on the bottle the volume of the breath.

4 The subject should then perform 2 minutes of gentle exercise, such as stepping up and down onto a bench.

5 Immediately after the exercise has finished measure the breath volume using the method described in Step 3. Also keep a note of the breaths per minute and the pulse rate.

Sample results

	Before exercise	After exercise
Breaths per minute	3	6
Volume in litres	1.9	3.2
Pulse in beats per minute	65	95

Data response questions

1 Why did the subject need to relax for a short while before taking the 'at rest' measurements?

2 What is the percentage increase in pulse rate before and after exercise?

3 What is the difference between the amount of air processed per minute before and after exercise?

Answers are on page 125.

Discussion

Even a fairly moderate increase in activity produces a rise in the rate and volume of breathing. The total difference in the volume of air processed is considerable given this doubling in the rate of breathing.

The pulse rates behave as expected. If the rate were monitored over time after the exercise there would be a gradual return to the resting rate. The time taken to return to this level is often regarded as a measure of fitness: the shorter the time required the fitter the individual.

QUESTIONS

Q1 Describe how the structure of the leaf is adapted for gas exchange.

Q2 a How many cells does oxygen pass through on its way from the alveoli to the red blood cells?
b Why is it important for there to be a large concentration gradient of oxygen between the inside of the alveoli and the blood?

Q3 When you breathe in, how do the positions of the diaphragm and ribcage change?

Q4 Why do we need rings of cartilage in the walls of the air passages?

More questions on the CD ROM

Answers are on page 160.

TRANSPORT

Videos & questions on the CD ROM

Simple unicellular organisms or organisms consisting of only a small number of cells can obtain all the nutrients and gases they require by simple diffusion, and excrete waste products in the same way. Their surface area, over which exchange with the external environment can occur, is large enough when compared to their total volume. In larger organisms the cells situated towards the centre would not receive all the nutrients they needed and excretion of waste products would be a problem unless some form of transport system were used.

Transport in flowering plants

In humans and many other animals, substances are transported around the body in the blood through blood vessels. In plants, water and dissolved substances are also transported through a series of tubes or vessels. There are two types of transport vessel in plants, called **xylem** and **phloem**.

Xylem vessels are long tubes made of the hollow remains of dead cells. They carry **water** and **dissolved minerals** up from the roots, through the stem, to the leaves. They also give **support** to the plant.

Phloem vessels are living cells. They carry **dissolved food materials**, mainly sucrose, but also substances such as amino acids, from the leaves to other parts of the plant, for example growing roots or shoots or storage areas such as fruit. This movement of food materials is called **translocation**.

In roots the xylem and phloem vessels are usually grouped together separately, but in the stem and leaves they are found together as **vascular bundles** or **veins**.

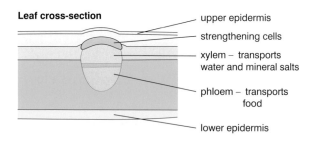

Leaf cross-section
- upper epidermis
- strengthening cells
- xylem – transports water and mineral salts
- phloem – transports food
- lower epidermis

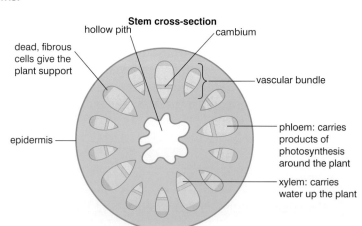

Stem cross-section
- hollow pith
- cambium
- dead, fibrous cells give the plant support
- vascular bundle
- epidermis
- phloem: carries products of photosynthesis around the plant
- xylem: carries water up the plant

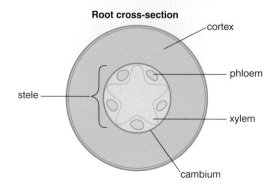

Root cross-section
- cortex
- phloem
- stele
- xylem
- cambium

HOW DO PLANTS GAIN WATER?

Roots are covered in tiny **root hair cells**, which increase the surface area for absorption. Water enters by **osmosis** because the solution inside the cells is more concentrated (has less water molecules) than the water in the soil.

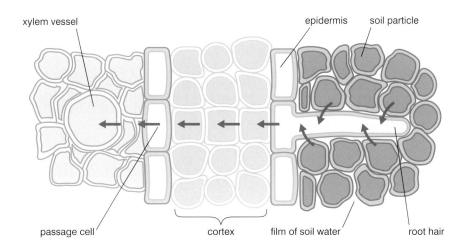

Water continues to move between cells by osmosis until it reaches the **xylem** vessels, which carry it up to the leaves.

HOW DO PLANTS LOSE WATER?

In the **leaves**, water moves out of the xylem and enters the leaf cells by osmosis (because the cells contain many dissolved substances). Water **evaporates** from the surface of the cells inside the leaf and then **diffuses** out through the open stomata. The evaporation of water causes more water to rise up the xylem from the roots rather like a drink flows up a straw when you suck at the top.

Water loss from the leaves is known as **transpiration**. The flow of water through the plant from the roots to the leaves is known as the **transpiration stream**.

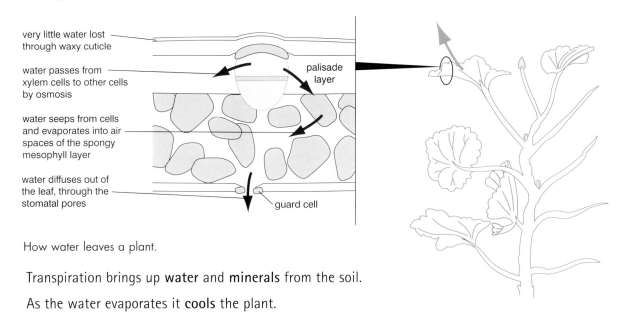

How water leaves a plant.

Transpiration brings up **water** and **minerals** from the soil.

As the water evaporates it **cools** the plant.

Transpiration happens faster in conditions that encourage evaporation, so when:

- it is warm
- it is windy
- it is dry
- it is very sunny (because this is when the stomata are most open)
- the plant has a good water supply.

EXPERIMENT TO INVESTIGATE TRANSPIRATION AND ENVIRONMENTAL CONDITIONS

Transpiration is the loss of water vapour from the aerial parts of a land plant. It occurs mainly through pores on the underside of the leaves called stomata. The process is passive and does not require an energy input by the plant. However, the plant can control its rate of transpiration to some extent by opening and closing these stomata in different conditions.

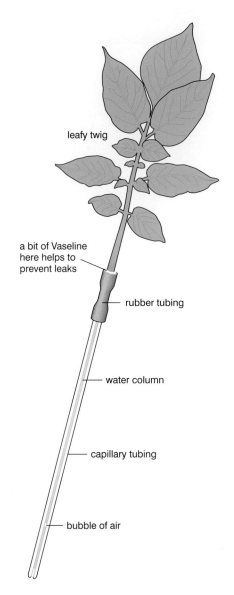

leafy twig

a bit of Vaseline here helps to prevent leaks

rubber tubing

water column

capillary tubing

bubble of air

You will need:

- Potometer
- Leafy twig
- Scalpel
- Water trough
- Vaseline or petroleum jelly
- Stopwatch or clock
- Fan or hairdryer

1 A potometer is used to measure the rate of water uptake of a leafy twig. It consists of a section of rubber tubing, which holds the twig and is connected to a length of capillary tubing. To prepare the twig, hold it underwater and cut a small length (about 3cm) from the bottom. Doing this underwater prevents air getting into the xylem vessels.

2 Insert the cut end of the twig into the rubber tubing of the potometer while keeping both underwater. Remove the potometer and twig from the water. If the water meniscus in the capillary tubing of the potometer moves very slowly towards the twig you have assembled the equipment correctly. Any other sort of movement indicates a leak. Try to plug this with Vaseline or re-insert the twig underwater.

3 Set up the potometer and time how long it takes for the water meniscus to travel a measured distance along the capillary tube.

4 Refill the capillary tube with water by squeezing on the rubber tubing while the end of the capillary is underwater. Then repeat Step 3 for various conditions as listed below. Use a fan or hairdryer to create the air current.

Sample results

Conditions	Time for water bubble to move 5cm, in seconds
Still air, sunlight	135
Moving air, sunlight	75
Still air, dark cupboard	257
Moving air, dark cupboard	122
Hot, moving air, sunlight	54

Data response questions

1 Which conditions produce the highest rate of transpiration?

2 How much faster in the highest rate of transpiration compared with the slowest rate?

3 Why do gardeners need to supply more water to their plants in hot, dry conditions than in cold, damp ones?

4 What would happen to the rate of movement of the bubble if air leaked into the rubber tubing?

Answers are on page 125.

Discussion

The conditions that produce the greatest transpiration from the leaves are hot, moving air in the sunlight. This is as expected given that sunlight opens the stomata and the hot moving air maintains a strong water vapour gradient around the leaves.

Transport in humans

Blood is the body's **transport system**, carrying materials from one part of the body to another. Some of the substances transported are shown in the table below.

Substance	Carried from	Carried to
Food (glucose, amino acids, fat)	Small intestine	All parts of the body
Water	Intestines	All parts of the body
Oxygen	Lungs	All parts of the body
Carbon dioxide	All parts of the body	Lungs
Urea (waste)	Liver	Kidneys
Hormones	Glands	All parts of the body (different hormones affect different parts)

The blood also plays a part in **fighting disease** and in **controlling body temperature**.

Parts of the blood	Job
Plasma (pale yellow liquid making up most of the blood)	Transports food, carbon dioxide, urea, hormones, antibodies and other substances all dissolved in water. Heat is also redistributed around the body
Red blood cells	Carry oxygen (and some carbon dioxide)
White blood cells	Defend body against disease
Platelets	Involved in blood clotting

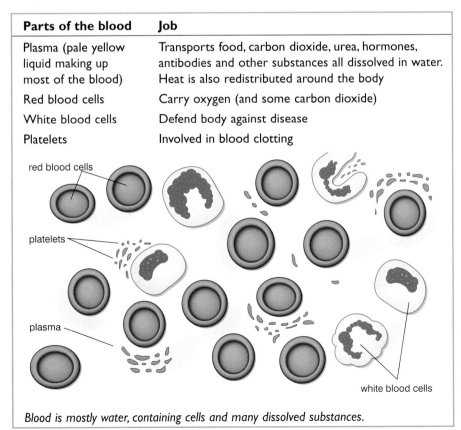

red blood cells

platelets

plasma

white blood cells

Blood is mostly water, containing cells and many dissolved substances.

A* EXTRA

- In the lungs, haemoglobin combines with oxygen to form oxyhaemoglobin.
- In other organs and tissues oxyhaemoglobin splits up into oxygen and haemoglobin.

There are different types of white blood cells that perform different jobs in preventing infection. Some cells take in and destroy invading microorganisms. Others are stimulated to produce antibodies specific to a particular pathogen.

Platelets also help to protect against disease. Clotting prevents the loss of blood but also seals a wound that could be the point of entry for infection.

Red blood cells are **specialised** to carry oxygen.

Feature of red blood cells	How it helps
'Biconcave' disc shape (flattened with a dimple in each side)	Large surface area for oxygen to enter and leave
No nucleus	More room to carry oxygen
Contains haemoglobin (red pigment)	Haemoglobin combines with oxygen to form oxyhaemoglobin. The oxygen is released when the cells reach tissues that need it
Small	Can fit inside the smallest blood capillaries. Small cells can quickly 'fill up' with oxygen as it is not far for the oxygen to travel right to the centre
Flexible	Can squeeze into the smallest capillary
Large number	Can carry a lot of oxygen

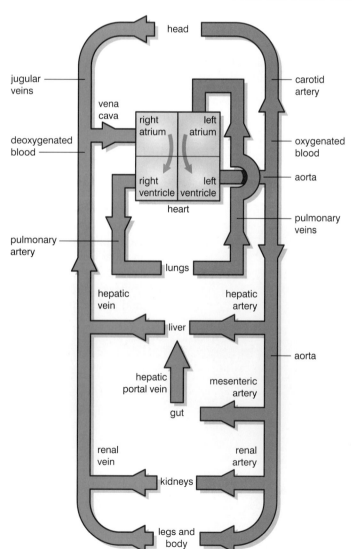

THE CIRCULATORY SYSTEM

Blood flows around the body through **arteries, veins** and **capillaries**. The **heart** pumps to keep the blood flowing.

In this micrograph you can see the distinctive biconcave shape of red blood cells.

THE HEART

The **heart** is a muscular bag that pumps blood by expanding in size, filling with blood, and then contracting, forcing the blood on its way.

The heart is two pumps in one. The right side pumps blood to the lungs to collect oxygen. The left side then pumps the **oxygenated blood** around the rest of the body. The **deoxygenated** (without oxygen) blood then returns to the right side to be sent to the lungs again.

The heart contains several valves and four chambers, two called atria (singular: atrium) and two called ventricles. The **atria** have thin walls. They collect blood before it enters the ventricles. The **ventricles** have thick muscular walls that contract, forcing the blood out. The **valves** allow the blood to flow one way only, preventing it flowing back the way it came.

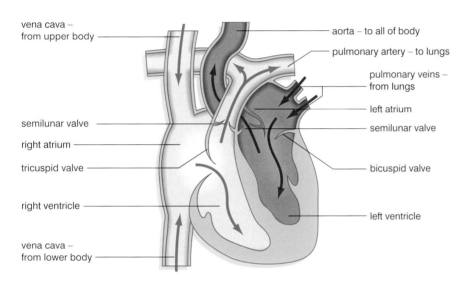

artery:
thick-walled carrying blood at high pressure

BLOOD VESSELS

Blood leaves the heart through **arteries** and returns through **veins**. **Capillaries** connect the two. Remember, **a** for **a**rteries that travel **a**way from the heart. **V**eins carry blood into the heart and contain **v**alves.

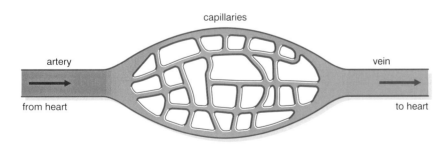

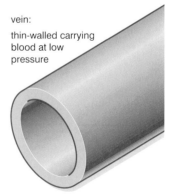

vein:
thin-walled carrying blood at low pressure

Arteries, veins and capillaries are adapted to carry out their different jobs.

Tissue fluid leaks from the capillaries. The tissue fluid bathes all the cells. Oxygen and other substances diffuse from the blood, through the tissue fluid to all of the cells. Waste substances such as carbon dioxide diffuse into the blood.

capillary:
very small; the walls may be just one cell thick

normal blood flow

open

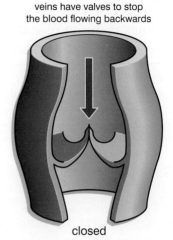
veins have valves to stop
the blood flowing backwards

closed

Blood vessel	Job	Adaptations	Explanation
Arteries	Carry blood away from heart	Thick muscular and elastic wall	Blood leaves the heart under high pressure. The thick wall is needed to withstand and maintain the pressure. The elastic wall gradually reduces the harsh surge of the pumped blood to a steadier flow
Veins	Carry blood back to the heart	Thinner walls than arteries	Blood is now at a lower pressure so there is no need to withstand it
		Large lumen (space in the middle)	Provides less resistance to blood flow
		Valves	Prevent back flow, which could happen because of the reduced pressure
Capillaries	Exchange substances with body tissues	Thin, permeable wall (may only be one cell thick)	Substances such as oxygen and food can enter and leave the blood through the capillary walls
		Small size	Can reach inside body tissues and between cells

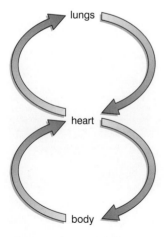

lungs

heart

body

The heart pumps blood to the lungs and back, then to the body and back. This is a double circulation.

DOUBLE CIRCULATION

In humans (but not all animals) the blood travels through the heart twice on each complete journey around the body. This is a **double circulation**.

By the time the blood has been pushed through a system of capillaries (in either the lungs or the rest of the body) it is at quite a low pressure. The pressure required to push the blood through the lungs and then the rest of the body in one go would be enormous and could damage the blood vessels. A double circulation system maintains the high blood pressure needed for efficient transport of materials around the body.

The double circulation also allows for the fact that the pressure needed to push blood through the lungs (a relatively short round trip) is much smaller than the pressure needed to push blood around the rest of the body. This is why the left half of the heart is much more muscular than the right half.

BLOOD PRESSURE

Your **blood pressure** is the measure of the pressure of your blood when your heart is contracting and relaxing.

Increases in blood pressure can be caused by:

- increases in the levels of carbon dioxide in the blood because of exercise.

- the action of adrenaline. Adrenaline is sometimes called the 'fight, flight or fright' hormone. It helps prepare the body for action by increasing the heart rate.

These increases in blood pressure increase the supply of oxygen to the tissues.

Too much salt in the diet can also raise blood pressure.

The heart rate is adjusted to try and maintain a constant blood pressure when the body is at rest.

Health risks are associated with blood pressure.

- People with high blood pressure could suffer a stroke. This may be caused by blood vessels in the brain bursting.

- People with low blood pressure may suffer with kidney problems, as the kidney loses its ability to filter blood.

QUESTIONS

Q1 a What are the differences between xylem and phloem?

Q2 Small organisms, like *Amoeba*, a single-celled organism, do not need a transport system. Why do bigger organisms need them?

Q3 This equation shows the reversible reaction between oxygen and haemoglobin.
oxygen + haemoglobin = oxyhaemoglobin
a Where in the body would oxyhaemoglobin form?
b Where in the body would oxyhaemoglobin break down?
c People who live at high altitudes, where there is less oxygen, have more red blood cells per litre of blood than people who live at lower altitudes. Suggest why.

Q4 a In the heart, the ventricles have thicker walls than the atria. Why is this?
b Why does the left ventricle have a thicker wall than the right ventricle?

Q5 a List three ways that veins differ from arteries.
b Substances such as oxygen and food enter and leave the blood through the capillary walls. Why do they not leave through the walls of arteries and veins?

More questions on the CD ROM

Answers are on page 160.

EXCRETION

Videos & questions on the CD ROM

Excretion is defined as the process or processes by which an organism eliminates the waste products of its chemical activities. Remember that this is different from egestion.

Excretion in flowering plants

In flowering plants the waste products that need to be excreted are carbon dioxide and oxygen. Carbon dioxide is produced in respiration while oxygen is a by-product of photosynthesis. These gases diffuse out of cells and are excreted through the stomata of the leaves.

Excretion in humans

The lungs, skin and kidneys are all organs of excretion in the human.

Water vapour and waste gases, mainly carbon dioxide, are excreted from the lungs.

Water and salt are excreted via the skin in the form of sweat.

As well as their role in the excretion of waste products a major function of the kidneys is osmoregulation, the control of water balance.

THE ROLE OF THE KIDNEYS

The amount of water that is lost from the body as urine is controlled by the **kidneys.**

The kidneys regulate the amounts of water and salt in the body by controlling the amounts in the blood.

The kidneys remove waste products such as **urea** from the blood. Urea is formed in the liver from the breakdown of excess amino acids in the body. This is an example of **excretion.**

As blood flows around the body it passes through the kidneys, which remove urea and excess water and salt from the blood.

1   Blood enters the kidneys through the **renal arteries**, which divide to form many **arterioles.** Each arteriole forms tiny capillaries that divide and coil, forming a **glomerulus.** The glomerulus is contained in a double-walled, cup-shaped structure called the Bowman's capsule, the first part of the kidney tubule.

2   A lot of the blood plasma is forced under great pressure into tiny tubules called **nephrons.** This process is called **ultrafiltration.** The glomerular filtrate produced is very similar in composition to the blood except that it does not contain blood cells or plasma proteins. It does contain glucose, amino acids, hormones, vitamins, salts, urea and water.

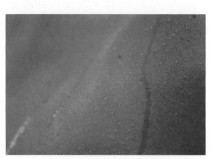
Sweat is water and salt that have been excreted from the body via the skin.

A* EXTRA

- A good understanding of the roles of the parts of the kidney nephron, and the role of ADH, is necessary for high marks.

3   The liquid moves along the nephron from the proximal convoluted tubule (where all the glucose in the filtrate is reabsorbed into the blood by active transport) round the hair-pin-shaped loop of Henlé to the distal convoluted tubule. This structure allows for the reabsorption of useful substances such as amino acids, hormones, vitamins, salts and water into the blood, leaving urea, excess water and excess salts. This mixture is called urine.

4   In the collecting duct more water is absorbed back into the blood, as needed by the body. The amount of water absorbed depends on the level of a hormone called anti-diuretic hormone (ADH). When ADH levels are high, lots of water is reabsorbed. When they are low little water is absorbed and large amounts of dilute urine is produced.

5   The capillaries join up to form the **renal veins**, which carry blood away from the kidneys.

6   The nephrons join up to form a **ureter**, which carries the urine to the bladder where it is stored until you go to the toilet, when the urine leaves the body through the **urethra**.

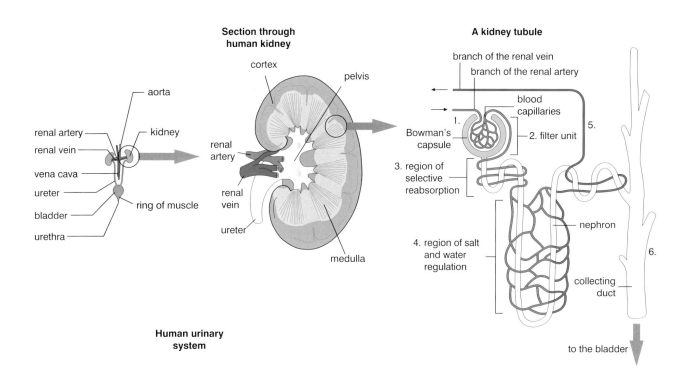

Section through human kidney

A kidney tubule

Human urinary system

MONITORING WATER BALANCE

Like temperature, the water content of the blood is monitored by the **hypothalamus.**

If there is too little water in the blood, for example if you have been sweating a lot, then the hypothalamus is stimulated and sends a hormone called **ADH** to the kidneys. This affects the collecting ducts, causing them to reabsorb more water back into the blood so that less is lost in urine. This is shown in the diagram below.

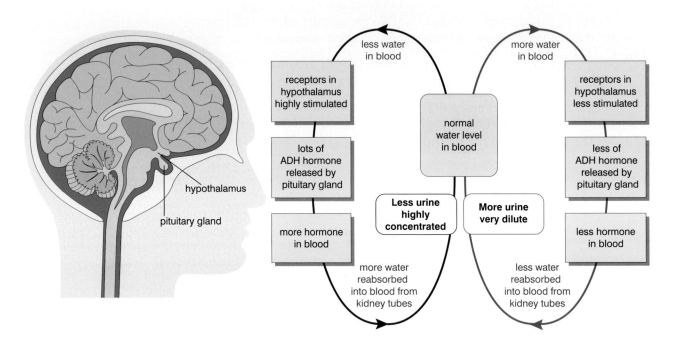

If your blood water level is high, for example if you have been drinking a lot, the hypothalamus is much less stimulated so less ADH is released, less water is reabsorbed and more water is lost in urine.

QUESTIONS

Q1 A farmer who has been working outside all day on a hot summer's day produces a much smaller amount of urine than normal. It is also a much darker yellow colour than normal. Explain these points.

Q2 Why are the lungs organs of excretion?

Q3 How would the blood in the renal arteries be different from the blood in the renal veins?

Answers are on pages 160–1.

More questions on the CD ROM

COORDINATION AND RESPONSE

Sensitivity, the ability to recognise and respond to changes in external and internal conditions, is recognised as one of the characteristics of living organisms.

A change in conditions is called a **stimulus**. For a coordinated response to occur to that stimulus there must be a **receptor** that can recognise the stimulus and an **effector**, a mechanism to carry out the response.

The internal environment of a mammal must be kept constant so that the best conditions for its body's functioning are maintained. The maintenance of this constant internal environment is termed homeostasis. The regulation of body water content and of body temperature are examples of homeostasis in action.

Coordination and response in flowering plants

TROPISMS

Tropisms are **directional growth responses** to stimuli.

Examples of tropisms include shoots growing towards the light and against the force of gravity, and roots growing downwards away from light but towards moisture and in the direction of the force of gravity. Growth in response to the direction of light is called **phototropism**. If the growth is towards light, it is called positive phototropism, as in shoots. Growth in response to gravity is called **geotropism**.

Tropisms are controlled by hormones called **auxins**. Auxin is made in the tips of shoots and roots and diffuses away from the tip before it affects growth. One effect of auxin is to inhibit the growth of side shoots. This is why a gardener who wants a plant to stop growing taller and become more bushy will take off the shoot tip, so removing a source of auxin.

The growth of **shoots** towards light can be explained by the behaviour of auxin. Auxin moves **away** from the lighter side of a plant to the darker side. Its presence on the darker side encourages growth by increasing cell elongation. The darker side then grows more than the lighter side, and the shoot bends towards the light source.

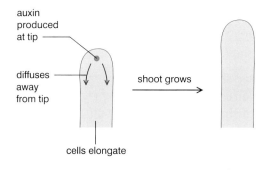

auxin produced at tip

diffuses away from tip

shoot grows

cells elongate

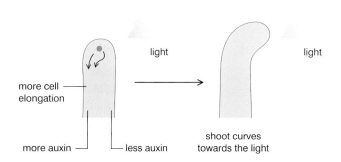

light

more cell elongation

more auxin — less auxin

light

shoot curves towards the light

In roots, gravity causes the auxin to collect on the **lower** side. Here it **stops** the cells elongating, which causes the root to bend downwards.

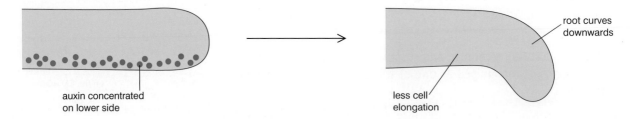

auxin concentrated on lower side

less cell elongation

root curves downwards

EXPERIMENT TO INVESTIGATE PHOTOTROPIC RESPONSES IN PLANTS

Light is necessary for the growth of green plants. If the available light is only coming from a particular direction the plant will grow to maximise the exposure of its leaves to this light.

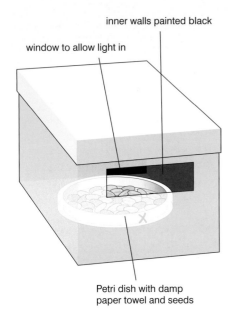

inner walls painted black

window to allow light in

Petri dish with damp paper towel and seeds

You will need:
- Cardboard box (with a lid) big enough to hold the Petri dish or tray
- Black paint or paper
- Petri dish or plastic tray for seeds
- Marker pen
- Paper towel
- Water
- Wheat or barley seeds

1 Paint the inside of the box black or line it with black paper. Cut a window out of one end to act as a light source. Make sure that light cannot get into the box other than through this window. The window must be big enough to let in a significant amount of light but not so big that it lights the end of the box furthest away from it.

2 Mark an X on one edge of the Petri dish. Place a thin layer of paper towel in the bottom of the dish and add water. Scatter about 40 seeds onto the moist towel.

3 Place the Petri dish in the box so that the only light falling onto the seeds comes from the window. The X on the dish should be nearest the window.

4 Leave the box for 48 hours and then check to see if the seeds have germinated. If the paper towel in the Petri dish is dry, you may need to add some more water.

5 Check the seeds every day and record any relevant observations. Remember to look for the X when you record your results and, if you move the Petri dish, always replace it with the X pointing towards the window.

6 As a control experiment, repeat the procedure but this time turn the Petri dish through 90 degrees every 12 hours. If the bending is caused by directional light, these seeds should grow vertically upwards.

The seedlings germinate and produce shoots that bend towards the light. This reaction is called a tropic response and is controlled by chemicals called auxins produced by the tip of the growing shoot. By putting coloured filters over the window and repeating the experiment with fresh seeds it is possible to investigate which particular wavelengths of light produce the most marked response.

EXPERIMENT TO INVESTIGATE GEOTROPIC RESPONSES IN PLANTS

Seeds are able to detect the direction of gravity and ensure that the root grows downwards into the soil and the shoot grows upwards towards the light. This simple experiment demonstrates this phenomenon.

before germination

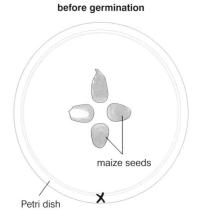

maize seeds

Petri dish   X

You will need:
- A Petri dish
- Maize seeds
- Paper towel
- Cotton wool
- Sticky tape
- A dark cupboard

1 Place four maize seeds in the middle of a Petri dish with the pointed ends facing outwards. Arrange the seeds so that they are aligned at 90 degrees to each other (like the four directions on a compass).

2 Place some paper towel gently over the seeds and then pack in some cotton wool on top of the paper towel. Use sufficient cotton wool that when you put the lid on the Petri dish, the seeds are held in place. Secure the lid with sticky tape.

3 Mark an X on the edge of the Petri dish. Place the Petri dish on its side in a dark cupboard with the X at the bottom. The seeds will start to germinate and produce shoots and roots.

4 Every day take the Petri dish out and record any observations about the size and growth direction of the roots. When you return the dish to the cupboard make sure that the X is always in the same position.

5 As a control experiment, repeat the procedure but this time turn the Petri dish through 90 degrees every 12 hours. If any growth effects are caused by the direction of the gravitational field these seeds should fail to exhibit them.

after a few days

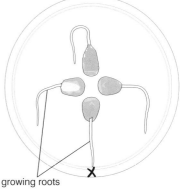

growing roots   X

The seedlings' roots all grow towards the centre of the Earth, even if this involves some strange growth patterns with roots bending.

A clinostat is a device that rotates a platform very slowly but continuously. It can be used to demonstrate the effect of gravity on root and shoot development. Small seedlings or germinating seeds are attached to the revolving platform of the clinostat. While the clinostat revolves (effectively exposing the plants to a continuously varying gravitational field) the seedlings grow horizontally. As soon as the clinostat is switched off the roots grow downwards while any shoots grow upwards.

Coordination and response in humans

There are two systems involved in coordination and response in humans.

One is the nervous system, which includes the brain, the spinal cord, the peripheral nerves and specialist sense organs such as the eye and the ear. Messages are passed around the nervous system in the form of electrical impulses and responses may be very rapid.

The other is the endocrine system, which uses chemical communication by means of hormones. Hormones are secreted by endocrine glands and act upon target cells. The endocrine system helps maintain basic body

A* EXTRA

- For the top grades you must be able to compare and contrast the two systems of coordination.

Sense organ	Sense	Stimulus
Skin	Touch	Pressure, pain, hot/cold temperatures
Tongue	Taste	Chemicals in food and drink
Nose	Smell	Chemicals in the air
Eyes	Sight	Light
Ears	Hearing	Sound
	Balance	Movement/ position of head

circular muscle relaxed

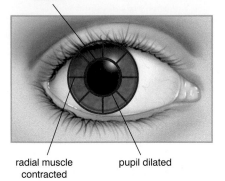

radial muscle contracted   pupil dilated

circular muscle contracted

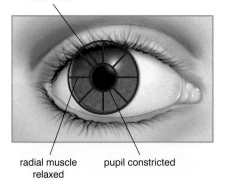

radial muscle relaxed   pupil constricted

functions including metabolism and growth. It often has more long-term effects than the nervous system and usually its response is less rapid.

The nervous system and the endocrine system work in conjunction in homeostasis.

THE NERVOUS SYSTEM

The **nervous system** collects information about changes inside and outside the body, decides how the body should respond and controls that response.

Receptors

Information is collected by **receptor cells**, which are usually grouped together in **sense organs**, also known as **receptors**.

Each type of receptor is sensitive to a different kind of change or **stimulus**.

The eye

The **eye** is the receptor that detects light.

The **iris** (ring-shaped, coloured part of the eye) controls the amount of light entering the eye by controlling the size of the hole in the centre, the **pupil**. The iris contains **circular** and **radial** muscles. In bright light the circular muscles contract and the radial muscles relax, making the pupil smaller. This reduces the amount of light entering the eye, as too much could do damage. The reverse happens in dim light, when the eye has to collect as much light as possible to see clearly.

The thick clear cornea bends light rays as they enter the eye in order to bring them to a focus on the retina. The lens provides fine focus to sharpen the image.

Rays of light from distant objects are almost parallel when they enter the eye. They require less bending and the cornea can manage most of it without help from the lens. Muscles in the ciliary body relax and the lens is pulled into a thinner shape by the suspensory ligaments. This provides the correct focussing power.

Rays of light from near objects are already diverging when they enter the eye. They need much more powerful refraction to bend them to a focus on the retina. Muscles in the ciliary body contract and the lens swells to a more rounded shape. This makes it more powerful and the rays are bent more to achieve a focussed image on the retina.

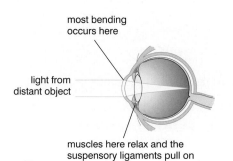

most bending occurs here

light from distant object

muscles here relax and the suspensory ligaments pull on the lens to make it thin and wide

rays are spread out so need more bending

light from near object

muscles in ciliary body contract, this reduces the tension on the lens which bulges to a fatter shape, which bends the light more

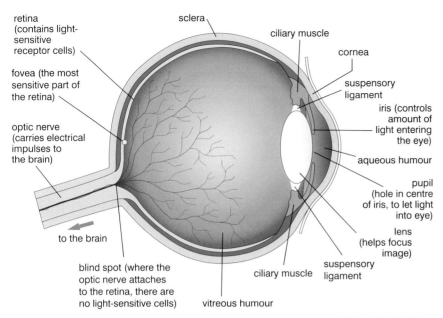

retina (contains light-sensitive receptor cells)

fovea (the most sensitive part of the retina)

optic nerve (carries electrical impulses to the brain)

to the brain

blind spot (where the optic nerve attaches to the retina, there are no light-sensitive cells)

vitreous humour

ciliary muscle

sclera

ciliary muscle

cornea

suspensory ligament

iris (controls amount of light entering the eye)

aqueous humour

pupil (hole in centre of iris, to let light into eye)

lens (helps focus image)

suspensory ligament

Part of eye	Job
Ciliary muscles	Contract or relax to alter the shape of the lens
Cornea	Transparent cover at front of the eye, allows light in and does most of the bending of light
Iris	Alters the size of the pupil to control the amount of light entering the eye
Lens	Changes shape to focus light on to the retina
Humour	Clear jelly that fills the inside of the eye and provides shape for the eye ball
Retina	Contains light-sensitive receptor cells, which change the light image into electrical impulses There are two types of receptor cells: **rods**, which are sensitive in dim light but can only sense 'black and white', and **cones**, which are sensitive in bright light and can detect colour
Sclera	Protective, tough outer layer
Suspensory ligaments	Hold the lens in position
Optic nerve	Carries electrical impulses to the brain

Central nervous system

The sense organs are connected to the rest of the **nervous system**, which is made up of the **brain, spinal cord** and **peripheral nerves**.

In the brain and spinal cord information is processed and decisions made. The brain and spinal cord together are called the **central nervous system (CNS)**.

The brain **coordinates** the actions of the body.

Different areas of the brain are responsible for different actions.

Signals are sent through the nervous system in the form of electro-chemical **impulses**.

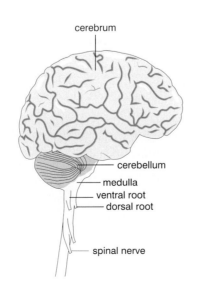

cerebrum

cerebellum

medulla

ventral root

dorsal root

spinal nerve

Areas of the brain.

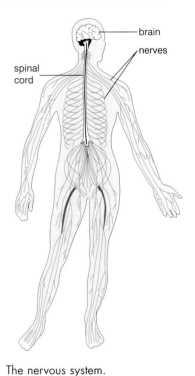

brain

nerves

spinal cord

The nervous system.

Types of nerve cells (neurones)

Nerve cells are called **neurones**.

Sensory neurones carry signals to the CNS.

Motor neurones carry signals from the CNS, controlling how the body responds.

Relay (intermediate or connecting) neurones connect other neurones together.

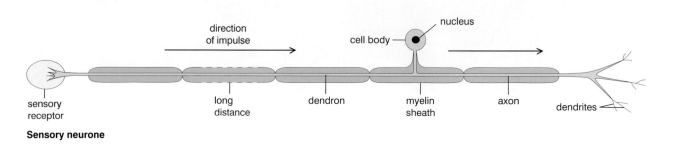

Sensory neurone

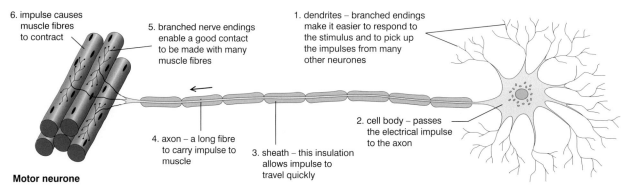

6. impulse causes muscle fibres to contract

5. branched nerve endings enable a good contact to be made with many muscle fibres

4. axon – a long fibre to carry impulse to muscle

3. sheath – this insulation allows impulse to travel quickly

2. cell body – passes the electrical impulse to the axon

1. dendrites – branched endings make it easier to respond to the stimulus and to pick up the impulses from many other neurones

Motor neurone

Relay neurone

Neurones are specialised

Neurones can be **very long** to carry signals from one part of the body to another.

Neurones have many branched nerve endings (**dendrites**) to collect and pass on signals. Nerve cells do not actually touch. There is a very small gap between them called a **synapse**. When an impulse arrives at the end of one neurone, chemicals are released which pass across this gap by diffusion. When they reach the other neurone, a new impulse is generated which passes along that neurone.

Many neurones are wrapped in a layer of fat and protein, the **myelin sheath**, which insulates cells from each other and allows the impulses to travel faster.

Neurones are usually grouped together in bundles called **nerves**.

Voluntary actions always involve the brain. When you run to kick a ball your brain will involve the memory while forming a response.

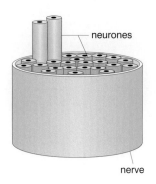

neurones

nerve

Cross-section of a nerve.

A* EXTRA

- For higher marks you will need to understand the structure and functioning of the reflex arc, and be able to interpret diagrams and describe what happens at each step.

Reflexes

The different parts of the nervous system may all be involved when your body responds to a stimulus. The simplest type of response is a **reflex**. Reflexes are rapid, automatic responses to a specific stimulus that often act to protect you in some way, for example blinking if something gets in your eye or sneezing if you breathe in dust.

The pathway that signals travel along during a reflex is called a **reflex arc**:

stimulus → receptor → sensory neurone → relay neurone in CNS → motor neurone → effector → response

Simple reflexes are usually **spinal reflexes**, which means that the signals are processed by the spinal cord, not the brain. The spinal cord sends a signal back to the **effector**. Effectors are the parts of the body that respond, either muscles or glands. Examples of spinal reflexes include standing on a pin or touching a hot object.

stand on pin → nerve endings → sensory neurone → spinal cord → motor neurone → leg muscles → leg moves

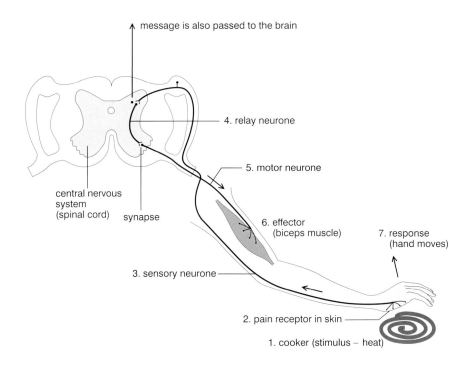

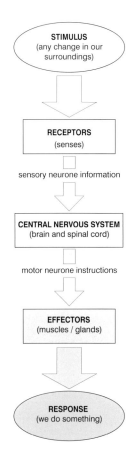

When the spine sends a signal to an effector, other signals are sent on to the brain so that it is aware of what is happening.

The flow of information from stimulus to response.

HOMEOSTASIS

For our cells to stay alive and work properly they need the conditions in and around them, such as the temperature and amount of water and other substances, to stay within acceptable limits. Keeping conditions within these limits, that is, keeping the internal environment constant, is called **homeostasis**.

The temperature inside your body is about 37°C, regardless of how hot or cold you may feel on the outside. This **core temperature** may naturally vary a little, but it never varies a lot unless you are ill.

Heat is constantly being **released** by respiration and other chemical reactions in the body, and is **transferred** to the surroundings outside the body. To maintain a constant body temperature these two processes have to balance. If the core temperature rises above or falls below 37°C various changes happen, mostly in the skin, to restore normal temperature.

Temperature control is a good example of negative feedback. In a negative feedback system any change will make the system respond in a way that minimises the change. So, if body temperature rises, the body responds by doing things that will tend to reduce temperature. Negative feedback is very common in biological systems. Blood sugar levels and water levels in the body are both controlled by negative feedback systems.

Too cold?	Too hot?
Vasoconstriction: blood capillaries in the skin become narrower so they carry less blood close to the surface. Heat is kept inside the body.	**Vasodilation:** blood capillaries in the skin widen so they carry more blood close to the surface. Heat is transferred from the blood to the skin by **conduction**, then to the environment by **radiation**.
Sweating is reduced.	**Sweating:** sweat is released onto the skin surface and as it evaporates heat is taken away.
Hair erection: muscles make the hairs stand up, trapping a layer of air as insulation (air is a poor conductor of heat). This is more beneficial in animals but still occurs in humans (goose bumps).	Hairs lay flat so less air is trapped and more heat is transferred from the skin.
Shivering: the muscle action of shivering releases extra heat from the increased respiration.	No shivering.
A layer of fat under the skin acts as **insulation**.	

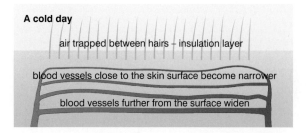

A cold day
air trapped between hairs – insulation layer
blood vessels close to the skin surface become narrower
blood vessels further from the surface widen

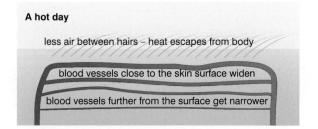

A hot day
less air between hairs – heat escapes from body
blood vessels close to the skin surface widen
blood vessels further from the surface get narrower

The core temperature is monitored by the **hypothalamus**: a part of the brain that monitors the temperature of the blood passing through it.

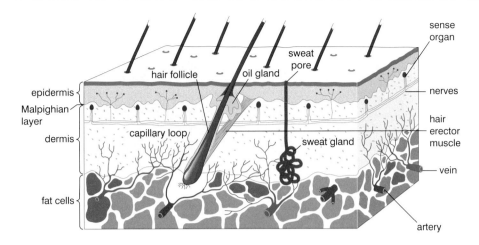

Section through skin.

HORMONES

Hormones are chemical messengers. They are made in **endocrine glands**.

Endocrine glands do not have ducts (tubes) to carry away the hormones they make: the hormones are **secreted directly into the blood** to be carried around the body in the blood plasma. (There are other types of glands, called exocrine glands, such as salivary and sweat glands, that do have ducts.)

Most hormones affect several parts of the body; others only affect one part of the body, called the **target organ**.

The changes caused by hormones are usually slower and longer-lasting than the changes brought about by the nervous system.

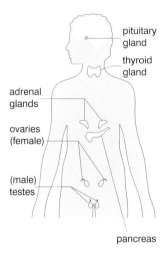

The endocrine system.

WHERE ARE HORMONES PRODUCED?

Adrenal glands

The **adrenal glands** produce **adrenaline**. This is released in times of excitement, anger, fright or stress, and prepares the body for 'flight or fight': the crucial moments when an animal must instantly decide whether to attack or run for its life.

The effects of adrenaline are:
- increased heart rate
- increased depth of breathing and breathing rate
- increased sweating
- hair standing on end (this makes a furry animal look larger but only gives humans goose bumps)
- glucose released from liver and muscles
- dilated pupils
- paling of the skin as blood is redirected to muscles.

Pituitary gland

The **pituitary gland** produces **growth hormone, anti-diuretic hormone (ADH)** and some other hormones.

Growth hormone helps physical development in children.

ADH causes the kidney tubules to reabsorb more water into the blood.

The pituitary gland also produces hormones which control many other glands such as FSH which controls oestrogen production in the ovaries.

Thyroid gland

The **thyroid gland** produces **thyroxine**.

Thyroxine helps mental and physical development in children.

Pancreas

The **pancreas** secretes **insulin** and **glucagon**. (It also secretes digestive enzymes through the pancreatic duct into the duodenum.)

Insulin controls the **glucose level** in the blood. It is important that the blood glucose level remains as steady as possible. If it rises or falls too much you can become very ill.

After a meal, the level of glucose in the blood tends to rise. This causes the pancreas to release **insulin**, which travels in the blood to the liver. Here it causes any excess glucose to be converted to another carbohydrate, **glycogen**, which is insoluble and is stored in the liver.

Between meals, glucose in the blood is constantly being used up, so the level of glucose in the blood falls. When a low level of glucose is detected, the pancreas stops secreting insulin and secretes the hormone **glucagon** instead. Glucagon converts some of the stored glycogen back into glucose, which is released into the blood to raise the blood glucose level back to normal.

Testes (males only)

Testosterone (the male sex hormone) is secreted from the **testes**. Testosterone causes secondary sexual characteristics in boys.

Ovaries (females only)

The **ovaries** produce the female sex hormones **progesterone** and **oestrogen**. Oestrogen is responsible for the development of secondary sexual characteristics in girls and together with progesterone it controls the menstrual cycle. (See page 83 for more details on the menstrual cycle.)

MEDICAL USES OF HORMONES

Hormones can be used to treat various medical conditions, for example illnesses caused by a hormone not being made naturally in the correct quantities.

Insulin

There are different types of diabetes, but in **diabetes mellitus** the body is unable to make enough of the hormone insulin. Insulin controls the level of glucose in the blood. Someone with diabetes cannot store excess glucose from their blood and it is excreted in urine instead. Other symptoms of diabetes include thirst, weakness, weight loss and coma.

Some people can control their diabetes with their diet and activity. For example, they make sure that they eat snacks between meals, eat some high-glucose food before any energetic activity and do not go for a long time without a meal.

Another way of controlling diabetes is to inject insulin before a meal.

Insulin can be extracted from animals' blood but is now produced by genetically engineered bacteria.

Controlling fertility

Contraceptive pills contain oestrogen and progesterone. They inhibit FSH production so that no eggs mature to be released.

FSH is used as a **fertility drug** to stimulate eggs to mature.

Growth hormone

Injections of growth hormone can be given during childhood to people that cannot produce enough of the hormone naturally, to ensure that growth is normal.

ILLEGAL USES OF HORMONES

Some drugs containing hormones, or chemicals similar to hormones, have been used by some athletes to **enhance their performance**. This is not only illegal but can have harmful side-effects.

QUESTIONS

Q1 Once a plant shoot has changed direction so it is growing towards the light, why does it stop bending?

Q2 **a** What is a stimulus?
b What is the difference between a receptor and an effector?

Q3 Signals can be sent round the body by the nervous system and the endocrine system. How are the two systems different?

Answers are on page 161.

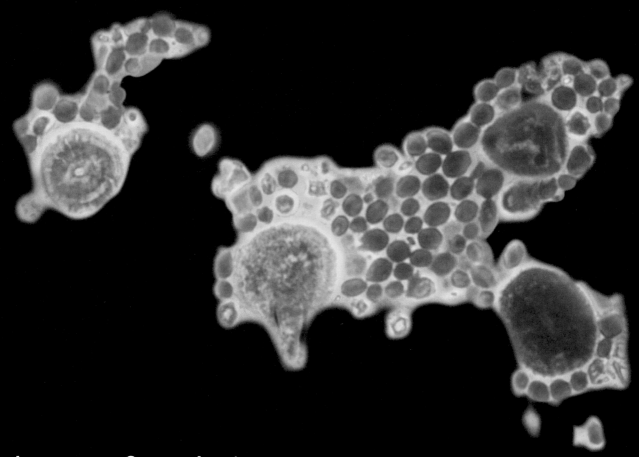

The power of reproduction

A single yeast cell can produce 20–30 exact copies of itself by budding. And each new cell can produce another 20–30 cells. In the right conditions, 1 g of yeast, which is less than a teaspoonful, can produce over 1000 tonnes of yeast in just a week. This reproduction is asexual and all the new cells are identical to the parent.

REPRODUCTION AND INHERITANCE

REPRODUCTION

Videos & questions
on the CD ROM

SEXUAL REPRODUCTION

Sexual reproduction is the most common method of reproduction for the majority of larger organisms, including almost all animals and plants. In sexual reproduction cell division occurs by a process called meiosis (see page 87). The cells produced by this process are called gametes and each gamete has only half the number of chromosomes of a normal cell of the species involved. To produce a new organism two gametes merge; this is known as fertilisation and the resulting cell is called a zygote.

Usually sexual reproduction involves two parent organisms of the same species. The zygote formed is genetically different from each of the parents. In some organisms self-fertilisation occurs but this is still sexual reproduction. Self-fertilisation occurs in many plants.

There are advantages and disadvantages to sexual reproduction.

Advantages
- Where genetic information is shared by gametes from two parents it produces variety in the offspring. This variety can then allow a species to evolve to exploit different environments.

Disadvantages
- Sexual reproduction usually requires a second parent for fertilisation. Finding a mate can have energy costs for the individual.

- It is a more complex procedure than asexual reproduction. There are more opportunities for things to go wrong.

ASEXUAL REPRODUCTION

Some organisms increase in number by asexual reproduction. For this type of reproduction it is not necessary to have two parents. During asexual reproduction new chromosomes are produced for the offspring by a process known as mitosis (see page 87). This is the same process that takes place during cell division for normal growth. The daughter cells produced by mitosis are genetically identical to the original cell. This means that organisms produced by asexual reproduction are genetically identical to their parents.

Like sexual reproduction, asexual reproduction has advantages and disadvantages.

Advantages
- Only one parent is required; there is no need for a parent animal to find a mate or for pollination as in plants.

- Often large numbers of organisms can be produced in a relatively short time.

- All the offspring produced are identical so should survive in the conditions in which the parent grows.

- Asexual reproduction is simple and reliable.

Disadvantages

- The lack of variation in the offspring means that any adverse change in conditions will affect all equally.

- Because the offspring do not vary they are not suited to moving away and exploiting environments with different conditions.

SEXUAL REPRODUCTION IN PLANTS

Flowering plants

The most successful group of plants is the flowering plants. These are the only plants to have true flowers and produce seeds with a tough protective coat. These adaptations allow flowering plants to reproduce sexually without a watery environment. When a flowering plant reproduces sexually it is able to:

- produce male and female gametes

- transfer the gametes between flowers

- fuse the gametes to produce a zygote

- produce seeds to protect the embryo from drying out and provide the new plant with food stores

- distribute seeds to new areas.

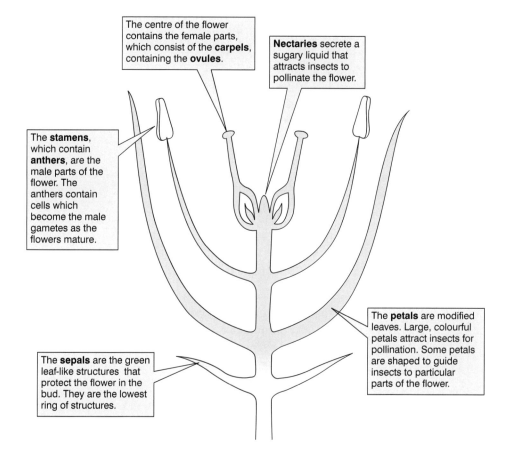

The centre of the flower contains the female parts, which consist of the **carpels**, containing the **ovules**.

Nectaries secrete a sugary liquid that attracts insects to pollinate the flower.

The **stamens**, which contain **anthers**, are the male parts of the flower. The anthers contain cells which become the male gametes as the flowers mature.

The **petals** are modified leaves. Large, colourful petals attract insects for pollination. Some petals are shaped to guide insects to particular parts of the flower.

The **sepals** are the green leaf-like structures that protect the flower in the bud. They are the lowest ring of structures.

Floral structure

All flowers have a similar basic arrangement. They have structures stacked one on top of each other along a short stem, arranged either in a spiral or in separate rings.

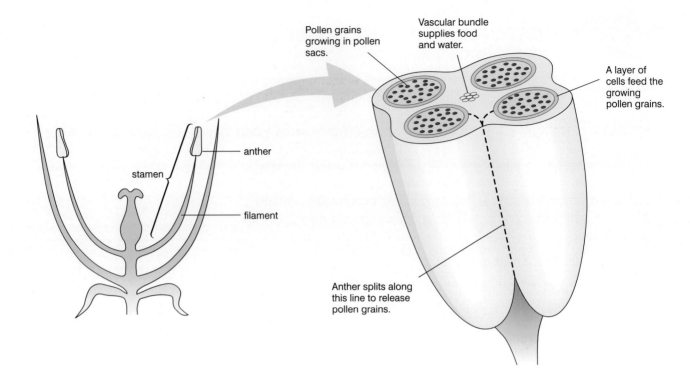

Pollen grains growing in pollen sacs.

Vascular bundle supplies food and water.

A layer of cells feed the growing pollen grains.

anther

stamen

filament

Anther splits along this line to release pollen grains.

The male parts

The male part of a flower is the ring of stamens. There may be up to 100 stamens, or fewer than a dozen. Each stamen consists of two parts - the anther at the top and a stalk called the filament.

The pollen grains contain the male gametes in flowering plants. Pollen develops in the pollen sacs of the anthers. Cells lining the inside of the pollen sacs divide by meiosis to give four cells. Each of these cells develops into a pollen grain. As the grains mature, they develop a thick outer wall to protect the delicate nuclei inside. When all the pollen grains in the anther are mature, the anther splits open to release them.

The female parts

The female part of the flower is the carpel, which produces the female gametes. A flower can contain more than one carpel, each with its own style and stigma. The stigma is the part of the carpel that collects the pollen.

The carpel is a bit like a hollow sac, which protects the female gamete from the dry air outside. The carpel contains one or more ovules and each ovule produces a single gamete by meiosis. The egg sac contains the nucleus, which will fuse with the pollen grain nucleus to form the zygote (the first nucleus of the new individual).

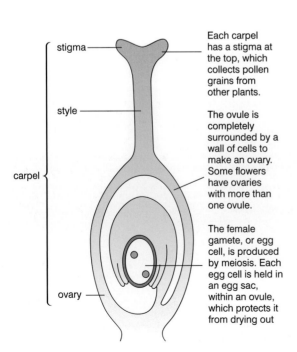

stigma

style

carpel

ovary

Each carpel has a stigma at the top, which collects pollen grains from other plants.

The ovule is completely surrounded by a wall of cells to make an ovary. Some flowers have ovaries with more than one ovule.

The female gamete, or egg cell, is produced by meiosis. Each egg cell is held in an egg sac, within an ovule, which protects it from drying out

Pollination

Different plants adapt the same basic pattern to produce very different-looking flowers. The adaptations are to do with the method of pollination. **Cross pollination** is the transfer of pollen from the stamen of one plant to the stigma of another. Most plants use either insect or wind pollination.

Wind-pollinated plants	Insect-pollinated plants
Have small petals, which do not obstruct pollen dispersal	Have large petals for insects to land on
Have green or inconspicuous petals	Have brightly coloured petals to attract insects
Have no scent	Are often scented to attract insects
Have no nectaries	Nectaries are present at the base of the flower. Nectaries produce a sugary liquid to attract insects, e.g. bees and butterflies
Have many anthers which are often large and hang outside the flower so that pollen is easily dispersed	Have a few small anthers which are usually held inside the flower
Pollen grains have smooth outer walls	Pollen grains have sticky or spiky outer walls
Stigmas are large and feathery, often hanging outside the flower to trap pollen	Stigmas are small and held inside the flower
Produce large amounts of pollen	Produce smaller amounts of pollen
Pollen is light	Pollen is heavier

Cross-pollination occurs when the pollen from one plant transfers to the stigma of a different plant. However, plants can produce both male and female gametes and it is possible for the pollen from one plant to pollinate its own stigma. This is called self-pollination. Most flowering plants try to prevent self-pollination by using self-incompatibility systems.

Some plants produce only flowers of a single sex, which makes self-pollination impossible. For example, pistachio trees are single sex.

Some plants have flowers that contain male and female parts, but the different parts mature at different times. For example, on a hemp plant the male flowers mature before the female. The female flowers mature before the male in the titan arum or bunga bangkai 'corpse flower' (*Amorphophallus titanum*).

Even if pollen from one flower manages to reach its own stigma, the pollen grain will tend to grow more slowly than a foreign grain. This means that nuclei from foreign pollen grains are more likely to fertilise the egg cell in the ovule.

Fertilisation

Pollination transfers pollen from anther to stigma. Fertilisation occurs when the nucleus from the pollen grain fuses with the nucleus in the egg sac. To get from the tip of the stigma to the egg sac, the pollen grain produces a thin tube called the pollen tube.

The zygote develops quickly to form an embryo plant, which needs to be protected from drying out. This embryo plant contains tissues that will become roots, stem and leaves when it starts to grow or germinate. Germination does not usually occur while the embryo is still attached to the parent plant. The embryo is said to be dormant. Flowering plants develop seeds to protect these embryo plants.

Seeds develop from the ovules. The wall of the carpel also develops to form a fruit. A pea pod shows the difference well as the peas are the seeds that contain the embryo plants, and the pod is the fruit.

In insect-pollinated plants, nectaries secrete a sugary liquid to attract insects.

These grass plants have anthers that hang outside the flowers and release large amounts of pollen to the wind. The stigmas also hang outside the flower to collect pollen from other grass plants.

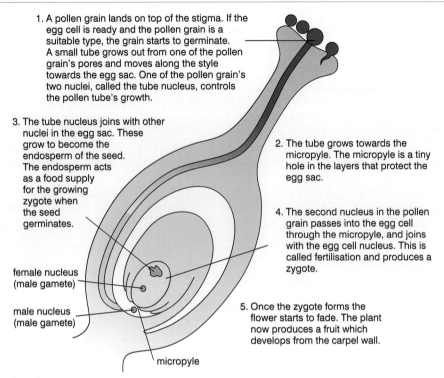

1. A pollen grain lands on top of the stigma. If the egg cell is ready and the pollen grain is a suitable type, the grain starts to germinate. A small tube grows out from one of the pollen grain's pores and moves along the style towards the egg sac. One of the pollen grain's two nuclei, called the tube nucleus, controls the pollen tube's growth.

3. The tube nucleus joins with other nuclei in the egg sac. These grow to become the endosperm of the seed. The endosperm acts as a food supply for the growing zygote when the seed germinates.

2. The tube grows towards the micropyle. The micropyle is a tiny hole in the layers that protect the egg sac.

4. The second nucleus in the pollen grain passes into the egg cell through the micropyle, and joins with the egg cell nucleus. This is called fertilisation and produces a zygote.

5. Once the zygote forms the flower starts to fade. The plant now produces a fruit which develops from the carpel wall.

female nucleus (male gamete)

male nucleus (male gamete)

micropyle

Seed structure

All seeds are formed containing food storage compounds in the endosperm. Endospermic seeds like wheat and rice contain a large store of endosperm at maturity. These are called endospermic seeds. In some plants, as the embryo plant develops the endosperm is used up to make large storage organs called cotyledons. These are called non-endospermic seeds and include plants like beans and peas. Plants with two cotyledons are called dicotyledenous plants.

The cotyledons are the first leaves of the embryo plant. They often do not look much like leaves; in peas they are so swollen that the pea is almost spherical in shape. Between the cotyledons is the embryo plant. The young root is called the radicle, the embryo shoot is the plumule.

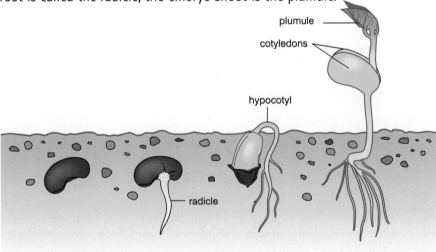

plumule

cotyledons

hypocotyl

radicle

Germination

Germinating seeds need a great deal of energy in a hurry because they need to mobilise their food reserves. This mobilisation uses enzymes that break down large carbohydrate molecules into smaller sugars. These sugars are respired to provide energy until the seedling is able to produce its own supply by photosynthesis.

Germination begins when the seed absorbs large amounts of water. The water helps to provide the right environment for the enzymes to work and to inflate the cells. As insoluble starch is broken down to soluble sugar, the water potential of the seed drops so even more water is drawn in by osmosis. The rate of respiration rises, needing a good supply of oxygen. This respiration tends to transfer some waste energy as heat, so germinating seeds warm up slightly.

Germination does not need light because germinating seeds are able to utilise food reserves until the seedlings can carry out photosynthesis. The germination of some seeds is inhibited by light.

ASEXUAL REPRODUCTION IN PLANTS

Many plants can reproduce by asexual reproduction, which may also be termed vegetative reproduction. The production of runners by some plants is a natural form of asexual reproduction, while the use of cuttings is an artificial method used in horticulture. The plants produced are genetically identical to the parent plants.

A runner grows out from the base of the parent plant along the ground until it reaches a suitable patch of earth a little distance from the parent. Here it develops roots. When the root system is sufficient, the stem connecting the new plant to the parent withers (e.g. strawberry plants).

A cutting is a piece that has been cut off from a mother plant and then rooted, often with the help of hormones in the form of a rooting powder. Cuttings can be taken as leaves, e.g. from African violets (*Saintpaulia*) or from stems, e.g. *Salvia*

Sexual reproduction in humans

MALE REPRODUCTIVE SYSTEM

The male has two testes. These are the organs in which sperm are produced. It is important that they are kept at a lower temperature than the rest of the body and so they are supported outside the body in the scrotum.

Testosterone (the male sex hormone) is secreted from the **testes**. Testosterone causes the following secondary sexual characteristics in boys:
- growth spurts
- hair growth on face and body
- penis, testes and scrotum growth and development
- voice breaking
- the body becoming broader and more muscular
- sexual 'drive' development.

The prostate gland and seminal vesicles together produce the liquid in which the sperm are able to swim. Semen is the mixture of sperm cells and fluids. Sperm ducts lead from the testes to the penis passing the prostate and seminal vesicles. The penis is used both to pass sperm into the vagina of the female and to carry urine out of the body. The urethra is the joint passage that takes both urine and sperm. A ring of muscle closes by reflex action on erection; this prevents sperm and urine being mixed up.

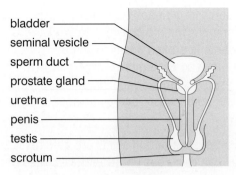

bladder
seminal vesicle
sperm duct
prostate gland
urethra
penis
testis
scrotum

The male reproductive system.

FEMALE REPRODUCTIVE SYSTEM

The two ovaries are the organs that produce the eggs. They are below the kidneys within the abdominal cavity, positioned either side of the uterus and joined to it by the oviducts.

The **ovaries** produce the female sex hormones **progesterone** and **oestrogen**. These hormones cause the following secondary sexual characteristics in girls:
- growth spurts
- breast development
- vagina, oviducts and uterus development
- menstrual cycle (periods) starting
- hips widening
- pubic hair and under-arm hair growth
- sexual 'drive' development.

These hormones also control the changes that occur during the **menstrual cycle**:
- oestrogen encourages the repair of the uterus lining after bleeding
- progesterone maintains the lining
- oestrogen and progesterone control ovulation (egg release).

The lower end of the uterus leads into the vagina, an elastic, muscular tube, at the cervix. The vagina opens at the vulva, which is formed by the meeting of folds of skin called the labia.

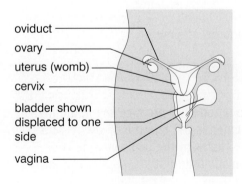

oviduct
ovary
uterus (womb)
cervix
bladder shown displaced to one side
vagina

The female reproductive system.

The menstrual cycle

About every 28 days an **egg** is released from one of a woman's ovaries. (The egg develops from one of the thousands of **follicles** present in the ovaries.) The egg travels down the **oviduct** to the **uterus** (womb) where, if it has been fertilised, it can implant and grow into a baby.

To prepare for possible fertilisation, the lining of the uterus thickens. This is controlled by the release of progesterone from the **corpus luteum,** the remains of the follicle left behind in the ovary. If the egg has not been fertilised then the lining breaks down and is released (**menstruation**). Oestrogen from the next follicle to mature will encourage the uterus lining to grow again for the next egg released.

If the egg has been fertilised, then progesterone continues to be released from the corpus luteum. This maintains the uterus lining during pregnancy and prevents further ovulation.

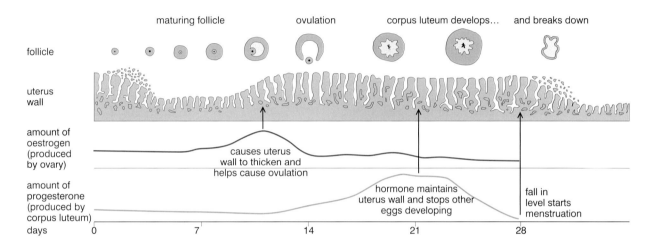

Sexual intercourse

The bringing together of the male and female gametes occurs during sexual intercourse.

Sperm deposited near the cervix swim up into the womb following a concentration gradient of chemicals produced by the female. These guide the sperm towards the egg. A number of sperm fail to make the journey but some will reach the oviducts at the top end of the womb. They must meet the egg here if fertilisation is to occur. The egg will have been travelling down from the ovary while the sperm have been swimming up from the womb.

Development of the fetus

After fertilisation in the oviduct, the fertilised egg or zygote travels on towards the uterus. The journey will take three days, during which time the zygote will grow from a single cell to a ball of 64 cells before it embeds itself in the uterus wall. Over the next 38 weeks it will increase its mass roughly 8 million times. At no other point in the individual's lifetime will it grow at such a high rate. This period of development in the uterus is known as gestation, and lasts about 40 weeks in humans, measured from the time of the woman's last period.

The rapid growth during gestation depends on a good supply of food and oxygen, provided by the mother.

Month of pregnancy	Development of fetus
0–3	Most of the key structures are laid down during this period. By the end of the third month the fetus can be recognised as male or female. It has a well-developed placenta linking it to the mother. The amnion has formed and surrounds the growing fetus with a bag of waters. The fetus is about 80mm long.
4–6	By 20 weeks the fetus is able to produce digestive enzymes and move itself. The mother will feel kicks from the baby by this stage.
7–9	The fetus grows in size but most of the key body parts have already developed. Babies born during this time can normally survive outside the mother although they will be small and will need special care. By the end of the ninth month the baby will weigh approximately 3–3.5kg. The placenta will weigh almost as much.

The placenta

The placenta is an organ that allows a constant exchange of materials between the mother and fetus. It develops from fetal tissues. The placenta and the uterus wall have a large number of blood vessels which run very close to each other but do not touch. Maternal and fetal blood do not mix. If they did, male children would be damaged by the level of female hormones in the mother's blood. The higher blood pressure in the mother could also damage the fetus. The fetus is a separate individual and has a completely different combination of antigens. If these antigens leaked into the mother's blood, she would produce antibodies that would attack the fetus.

Despite the blood not being allowed to mix, food, oxygen and waste materials pass rapidly across the placenta. The umbilical cord is the connection between the growing fetus and the placenta. After birth, the point where the cord joins to the baby constricts and the cord degenerates. All that is left of this important lifeline in later life is the 'belly button' or umbilicus.

The fetus develops inside a bag of fluid that protects it from mechanical damage. This fluid is called amniotic fluid and is produced from the amniotic membrane that forms the outer layer of the bag. One of the signs that birth is imminent is when this bag bursts during labour.

QUESTIONS

Q1 a Where is testosterone produced?
   b What secondary sexual characteristics does it cause?

Q2 When an egg has been fertilised:
   a what hormone prevents the lining of the uterus from breaking down?
   b from where is it released?

Q3 How is the developing baby protected:
   a from antibody attack from the mother?
   b from physical damage?

More questions on the CD ROM

Answers are on page 161.

INHERITANCE

No two people are the same. Similarly, no two trees (even if they are of the same species) will be exactly the same in every way, they will have different heights, different trunk widths and different numbers of leaves.

There are two types of variation:

1 **discontinuous variation** (sometimes called discrete variation) – a characteristic can have one of a certain number of specific alternatives, for example gender, where you are either male or female, and blood groups, where you are either A, B, AB or O

2 **continuous variation** – a characteristic can have any value in a range, for example body weight and length of hair.

CAUSES OF VARIATION

Environmental causes include your diet, the climate you live in, accidents, your surroundings, the way you have been brought up and your lifestyle. They all influence your characteristics.

Genetic causes are the characteristics controlled by your genes. Genes are inherited from your parents. Examples of characteristics in humans influenced purely by genes are eye colour and gender.

Many characteristics are influenced by environment **and** genes. For example people in your family might tend to be tall, but unless you eat correctly when you are growing you will not become tall, even though genetically you have the tendency to be tall. Other examples are more controversial, such as human intelligence, where it is unclear whether the environment or genes is more influential.

GENES

Genes are chemical **instructions** that direct the processes going on inside cells. They affect the way cells grow and work and so can affect features of your body such as the shape of your face and the colour of your eyes. All the information needed to make a fertilised egg grow into an adult is contained in its genes.

Inside virtually every cell in the body is a **nucleus**, which contains long threads called **chromosomes**. These threads are usually spread throughout the nucleus, but when the cell splits they gather into bundles that can be seen through a microscope. The chromosomes are made of a chemical called **deoxyribonucleic acid (DNA)**.

DNA is a very long molecule that contains a series of chemicals called **bases**. There are four different types of base in DNA: **thymine (T)**, **adenine (A)**, **guanine (G)** and **cytosine (C)**. C and G always match together and A and T always match together. The order in which the bases occur is a **genetic code**. The code spells out instructions that control how the cell works. Each length of DNA that spells out a different instruction is known as a **gene**. Each chromosome contains thousands of genes.

A* EXTRA

- DNA is made of very long strings of four different chemical bases.
- Each group of three bases codes for a particular amino acid, so the sequence of bases in a gene codes for the sequence of amino acids in a protein.

All the genes in a particular organism are known as its **genome**.

Genes tell cells how to make different **proteins**. Many proteins are enzymes that control the chemical processes inside cells.

Only some of the full set of genes are used in any one cell.

Most of our features that are controlled genetically are affected by several genes.

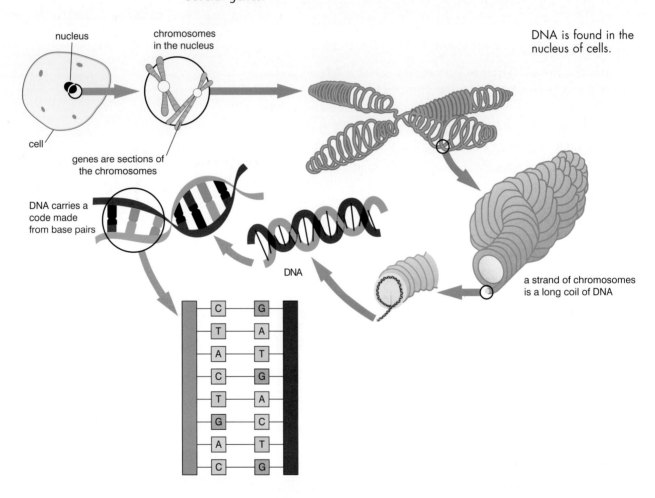

nucleus

cell

chromosomes
in the nucleus

genes are sections of
the chromosomes

DNA carries a
code made
from base pairs

DNA

DNA is found in the
nucleus of cells.

a strand of chromosomes
is a long coil of DNA

MUTATIONS

Sometimes genes can be altered so that their message becomes meaningless or a different instruction. This is known as a **mutation**: a rare, random change in genetic material that can be inherited. Spontaneous mutations are rare and the changes that occur in the genes are quite random.

The chance of a mutation occurring can be increased by:

- radiation, e.g. gamma rays, x-rays and ultraviolet rays

- certain chemicals, called **mutagens**, e.g. some of the chemicals found in tobacco.

Most mutations are harmful. Some mutations have neutral effects and a few mutations are beneficial to the plant or animal. Due to natural selection, the number of animals with a beneficial mutation will increase.

A single mutated gene causes the inherited disease **cystic fibrosis**.

An extra chromosome causes **Down's syndrome**. A person with Down's syndrome has 47 chromosomes per cell instead of the usual 46.

Mutations that occur in **sex cells** can be passed on to offspring, who may develop abnormally or may die at an early stage of development.

If mutations occur in **body cells** they may multiply uncontrollably. This is **cancer**.

CELL DIVISION

Cells grow by splitting in two. This is called **cell division**, and is used in normal body growth and repair. It is also the way that single-celled organisms reproduce and is the only type of cell division involved during **asexual reproduction** (reproduction that does not involve sex cells). It is also the form of reproduction used in cloning.

Before a cell splits, its chromosomes **duplicate** themselves. The new cells formed, sometimes called the **daughter cells**, contain chromosomes identical with the original cell. This type of cell division, in which the new cells are genetically identical to the original, is known as **mitosis**. Cells or organisms that are genetically identical to each other are known as **clones**.

Mitosis takes place in all the normal body cells.

A spider plant forms new plants at the end of stalks ('runners'). These new plants eventually grow independently of the parent plant. This is an example of asexual reproduction.

 Stage 1. The chromosomes get fatter and become visible.

 Stage 2. Each chromosome makes an exact copy of itself.

Stage 3. Remember that each chromosome has its own 'partner'. They carry similar 'blueprints' – one from the original father and one from the mother. These partner chromosomes get together and line up across the middle of the cell.

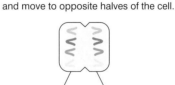 Stage 4. The colour chromosomes part and move to opposite halves of the cell.

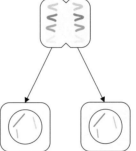 Stage 5. The cell splits in two. These new cells have the same number of chromosomes as the cell at the start of the process.

There is another type of reproduction in which the new individuals have been formed by two special cells, called **sex cells** or **gametes**, usually one from each parent. This type of reproduction is called **sexual reproduction**.

During sexual reproduction, a different type of cell division called **meiosis** makes sure that the gametes only have half the number of chromosomes that body cells have. In humans the gametes are **sperm** cells and **egg** cells. In flowering plants the gametes are the **pollen** cells and the female 'egg' cells (**ovules**).

The gametes contain half the normal number of chromosomes so that when they join together (at **fertilisation**) the normal number is restored. For example, human cells normally contain 23 pairs of chromosomes: 46 in total (**diploid number**). Human egg and sperm cells contain only 23 chromosomes (**haploid number**), so when they join together the new cell formed has the normal 46. (The number of chromosomes depends on an organism's species.) The random fusion of male and female gametes contributes to the genetic variation of offspring.

A* EXTRA

- In meiosis, cells divide twice, forming four gametes (sex cells), each with a single set of chromosomes. The new cells are not genetically identical.
- In mitosis, cells divide once, producing two cells, each with a full set of chromosomes. The new cells are genetically identical to each other and to the original cell.

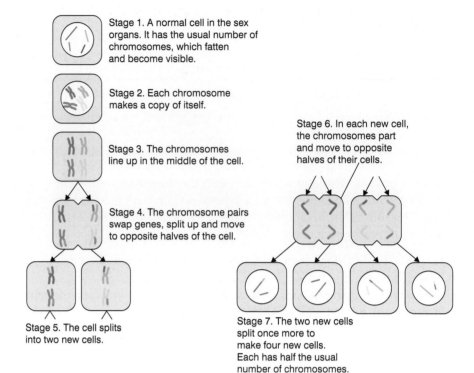

Stage 1. A normal cell in the sex organs. It has the usual number of chromosomes, which fatten and become visible.

Stage 2. Each chromosome makes a copy of itself.

Stage 3. The chromosomes line up in the middle of the cell.

Stage 4. The chromosome pairs swap genes, split up and move to opposite halves of the cell.

Stage 5. The cell splits into two new cells.

Stage 6. In each new cell, the chromosomes part and move to opposite halves of their cells.

Stage 7. The two new cells split once more to make four new cells. Each has half the usual number of chromosomes.

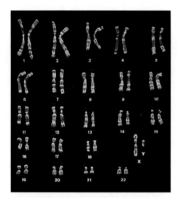

The 23 pairs of chromosomes in a human cell, including the X and tiny Y.

The offspring produced by sexual reproduction are genetically **different** from their parents.

Every gamete formed has one of each pair of chromosomes. However, which one of each chromosome pair ends up in a particular gamete is purely random. An individual human can produce gametes with billions of different combinations of chromosomes.

Added to this variation is the fact that when chromosome pairs are lying next to each other they swap lengths of DNA (**crossing over**), altering the combination of genes on a chromosome. It is therefore not surprising that, even with the same parents, we can look very different from our brothers and sisters.

HOW FEATURES ARE PASSED ON

Some features, such as the colour of your eyes, are passed on (**inherited**) from your parents, but other features may not be passed on. Sometimes features appear to miss a generation, for instance you and your grandmother might both have ginger hair, but neither of your parents do.

Dominant and recessive alleles

Leopards occasionally have a cub that has completely black fur instead of the usual spotted pattern. It is known as a black panther but is still the same species as the ordinary leopard.

Just as in humans, leopard chromosomes occur in **pairs**. One pair carries a gene for fur colour. There are two copies of the gene in a normal body cell (one on each chromosome). Both copies of the gene may be identical but sometimes they are different, one being for a spotted coat and the other for a black coat. Different versions of a gene are called **alleles**.

Leopard cubs receive half their genes from each parent. Eggs and sperm cells only contain half the normal number of chromosomes as normal body cells. This means that egg and sperm cells contain only one of each pair of alleles. When an egg and sperm join together at fertilisation the new cell formed, the **zygote**, which will develop into the new individual, now has two alleles of each gene.

Different combinations of alleles will produce different fur colour:

> spotted coat allele + spotted coat allele = spotted coat
>
> spotted coat allele + black coat allele = spotted coat
>
> black coat allele + black coat allele = black coat

The black coat only appears when **both** of the alleles for the black coat are present. As long as there is at least one allele for a spotted coat, the coat will be spotted because the allele for a spotted coat overrides the allele for a black coat. It is the **dominant allele**. Alleles like the one for the black coat are described as **recessive**.

Characteristics caused by two identical alleles are called **homozygous**.

Characteristics caused by two different alleles are called **heterozygous**.

Monohybrid crosses

An individual's combination of genes is his or her **genotype**. An individual's combination of physical features is his or her **phenotype**. Your genotype influences your phenotype.

We can show the influence of the genotype in a **genetic diagram**. In a genetic diagram we use a **capital letter** for the **dominant** allele and a **lower case letter** for the **recessive** allele.

Using the example of the leopards, the letter S stands for the dominant allele for a spotted coat and letter s stands for the recessive allele for the black coat. Two spotted parents who have a black cub must each be carrying an S and an s. The genetic diagram below shows the different offspring that may be born.

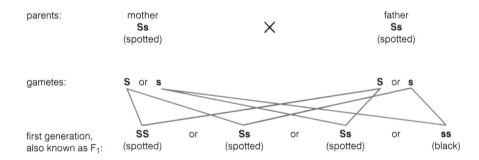

If the first generation, F_1, was crossed again, the offspring of this second generation would be referred to as F_2.

Because we are looking at only one characteristic (fur colour), this is an example of a **monohybrid cross**. 'Mono' means one, and a 'hybrid' is produced when two different types breed or cross.

Another type of genetic diagram is known as a **Punnett square**.

		male gametes	
		S	**s**
female gametes	**S**	**SS** (spotted)	**Ss** (spotted)
	s	**Ss** (spotted)	**ss** (black)

The example above can be shown in a Punnett square:

In a diagram of a monohybrid cross, when two heterozygous parents are crossed, the offspring that have the feature controlled by the dominant allele and the offspring that have the feature controlled by the recessive allele appear in a **3:1 ratio**. This is because of the random way that gametes combine. The 3:1 ratio refers to the **probabilities** of particular combinations of alleles, so, for example, there is a 1 in 4 chance of a leopard cub being black. SS and Ss are the genotypes for spotted leopards while ss will be for the black cub.

With a large number of offspring in an actual cross of two heterozygous leopard parents, you would expect something near the 3:1 ratio of spotted to black cubs. However, because it does only refer to probabilities you should not be too surprised if, for example, in a litter of four, two of the cubs were black or none was black.

Using the example of leopard coat colour and a Punnet square we can look at what happens if we cross homozygous and heterozygous individuals:

		male gametes	
		S	**s**
female gametes	**s**	**Ss**	**ss**
	s	**Ss**	**ss**

In the example above a black-coated leopard, homozygous ss, has been crossed with a heterozygous spotted coat leopard, Ss. If they produced four cubs then it is likely that two cubs would be heterozygous Ss and have spotted coats and two cubs would be homozygous ss and be black. The probable ratio of Ss individuals with the spotted coat phenotype to ss individuals with black coat phenotype would be 1:1.

Can you predict what will happen if a homozygous spotted coat leopard is crossed with a heterozygous spotted coat leopard?

male gametes

	S	S
S	SS	SS
s	Ss	Ss

female gametes

In this case, although some of the cubs born are likely to be homozygous and some heterozygous they will all have spotted coats. Phenotypically they will all be the same although genotypically they will be different.

The genotypes of individuals can be worked out by using a **family tree**.

CODOMINANCE

In the leopard example above, one allele of the gene pair for coat colour was dominant and the other was recessive. When both alleles of a gene pair in a heterozygote are expressed, with neither being dominant or recessive to the other, this is called codominance.

Human blood types are determined by three different alleles: I^A, I^B and I^O. The I^O allele is recessive but the I^A and I^B alleles are codominant. These three possible alleles can give us the following allele pairs:

- $I^A I^A$
- $I^B I^B$
- $I^O I^O$
- $I^A I^B$
- $I^A I^O$
- $I^B I^O$

These six different genotypes give us four different phenotypes: the four different human blood groups A, B, AB and O.

Blood group A can have $I^A I^A$ or $I^A I^O$ allele pairs (because I^A is dominant over recessive I^O).

Blood group B can have $I^B I^B$ or $I^B I^O$ allele pairs (because I^B is dominant over recessive I^O).

Blood group AB has the two codominant alleles, $I^A I^B$.

Blood group O has $I^O I^O$, the recessive pair.

Genes present	Blood group (phenotype)
$I^A I^A$	A
$I^A I^O$	A
$I^B I^B$	B
$I^B I^O$	B
$I^A I^B$	AB
$I^O I^O$	O

The genetic cross below shows how particular blood groups can be inherited.

Parent	Mother	Father	Notes
Genes present	$I^A I^B$	$I^O I^O$	Remember – two genes in all normal body cells
Blood group	$I^A I^B$	I^O	
Possible gametes	I^A or I^B	I^O	Since the genes are the same there is only one possible gamete for each parent.
Possible combinations	$I^A I^O$ or $I^B I^O$		It does not matter if you write the combination as $I^A I^O$ or $I^O I^A$, the important thing is which genes are present.
Blood groups	A or B		There is theoretically a 1:1 ratio of blood groups produced in the children from these parents.

INHERITED DISEASES

Some diseases or disorders can be inherited. Examples include:

- **cystic fibrosis** – in which the lungs become clogged up with mucus

- **haemophilia** – in which blood does not clot as normal

- **diabetes** – in which insulin is not made in the pancreas

- **sickle-cell anaemia** – in which the red blood cells are misshapen and do not carry oxygen properly

- **Huntington's disease** – a disorder of the nervous system.

Most inherited diseases are caused by **faulty genes**. For example, one form of diabetes is caused by a fault in the gene carrying the instructions telling the pancreas cells how to make insulin.

	male gametes	
	N	**n**
N	**NN** (makes insulin)	**nN** (makes insulin)
n	**Nn** (makes insulin)	**nn** (has diabetes)

female gametes

Most of these faulty alleles are **recessive**, which means that you have to have two copies of the faulty allele to show the disorder. Many people will be **carriers**, having one normal allele as well as the faulty version. The diagram (left) shows how two carrier parents could have a child with a disorder. The probability of these parents having a child with diabetes is a 1 in 4 chance, or 25 per cent.

SEX DETERMINATION

Whether a baby is a boy or a girl is decided by one pair of chromosomes called the **sex chromosomes**. There are two sex chromosomes, the X chromosome and the Y chromosome. Boys have one of each and girls have two X chromosomes.

	male gametes	
	X	**Y**
X	**XX** (girl)	**XY** (boy)
X	**XX** (girl)	**XY** (boy)

female gametes

Egg cells always contain **one X chromosome** but **sperm** cells have an equal chance of containing **either** an X chromosome **or** a Y chromosome. This means that a baby has an equal chance of being either a boy or a girl. This is shown in the diagram on the left.

SEX-LINKED INHERITANCE

Some genetic disorders, such as red–green colour blindness, are more common in men than women. The recessive allele causing the disorder is found on part of the X chromosome, and there is no equivalent part on the Y chromosome, because it is smaller (see the photograph on page 88), to carry either a dominant or recessive allele. This means that males only need to have one copy of the recessive allele to show the disorder, while females would need two copies.

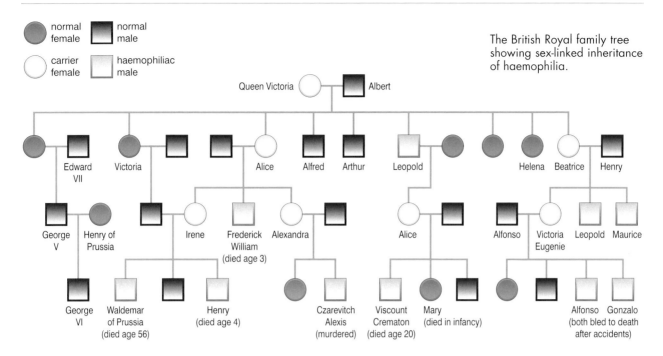

normal female
normal male
carrier female
haemophiliac male

The British Royal family tree showing sex-linked inheritance of haemophilia.

Queen Victoria — Albert

Edward VII · Victoria · Alice · Alfred · Arthur · Leopold · Helena · Beatrice · Henry

George V · Henry of Prussia · Irene · Frederick William (died age 3) · Alexandra · Alice · Alfonso · Victoria Eugenie · Leopold · Maurice

George VI · Waldemar of Prussia (died age 56) · Henry (died age 4) · Czarevitch Alexis (murdered) · Viscount Crematon (died age 20) · Mary (died in infancy) · Alfonso Gonzalo (both bled to death after accidents)

1 How do we know that Queen Victoria was a carrier for haemophilia even though her blood clotted normally?

- Because Albert was normal. If he had had the gene he would have suffered from haemophilia. Since the gene appeared in the children it must have come from Victoria.

2 Why was Leopold's daughter bound to be a carrier for haemophilia?

- She was bound to have the X-chromosome from Leopold. Since Leopold suffered from the disease she was bound to have the gene. If her mother had also been a carrier and both of her clotting genes had been the haemophilia form she would have died before birth as the double recessive is a fatal combination.

3 Can we be absolutely sure that Edward VII's wife was not a carrier of the haemophilia gene from this pedigree table?

- Not from the evidence in the table. She could have been a carrier but have passed on a healthy gene to George V.

4 If Victoria was X^hX and Albert was XY what were the genotypes for Leopold, Beatrice and Alfred?

- Leopold? X^hY
- Beatrice? X^hX
- Alfred? XY

QUESTIONS

Q1 Bob and Dave are identical twins. Dave emigrates to Australia, where he works outside on building sites. Bob stays in England and works in an office. Suggest how they might look (a) similar and (b) different. Explain your answers.

Q2 Put the following in order of size, starting with the smallest: cell nucleus, chromosome, gene, cell, chemical base.

Q3 In humans, the gene that allows you to roll your tongue is a dominant allele. Use a genetic diagram to show how two 'roller' parents could have a child who is a 'non-roller'.

Answers are on pages 161–2.

What a whopper!

The Rafflesia species produce the biggest flower of any plant on Earth. A single flower can be up to a metre in diameter, and weigh up to 10 kg! The plant is a parasite – its roots grow within vines that hang down from rain forest trees and trail along the ground and it is from the bark of this vine that the flower bud emerges. The flower quickly becomes colonised by flies, which in turn attract spiders and other insect eaters and is also the food of the squirrel-like tree shrew, which in fact is neither shrew-like nor a tree dweller but belongs to the primate family.

Rafflesia has a reputation of smelling like rotting flesh, although this may only be when it starts to die. The Indonesian name, bunga patma, means lotus flower, a symbol of fertility

Chapter 4

ECOLOGY AND THE ENVIRONMENT

Rafflesia keithii is a parasitic plant. It spends most of its life as a tiny thread within its host vine. The flower shows only when the plant reaches maturity, and lasts for just a few days

THE ORGANISM IN THE ENVIRONMENT

SOME ECOLOGICAL TERMS

The environment is important to every living thing. We need to understand and protect our environment.

Ecology is the study of how living things affect and are affected by other living things as well as by other factors in the environment.

An **ecosystem** is a community of species and their environment, for example the species in a pond.

Environment is a term often used to refer only to the physical features of an area, but can include living creatures.

A **community** means the different species in an area, for example all the species in a grassland.

A **species** is one type of organism, for example a robin. Only members of the same species can breed successfully with each other.

Population means the numbers of a particular species in an area or ecosystem.

An organism's **niche** is its way of life or part it plays in an ecosystem.

An organism's **habitat** is where an organism lives.

QUADRAT

A **quadrat** can be used to carry out a **plant survey**, for example to compare the plant life in two different areas. The quadrat is placed randomly a number of times in each area, and each time the plants within the quadrat are identified and counted. You then combine the results to find the average for each area.

If the area of the region being investigated and the area of the quadrat are both known, then an estimate can be made of the total numbers of each species. Using quadrats in this way is called **sampling**, because only a sample of the region is inspected. Inspecting every plant throughout the region would take too long.

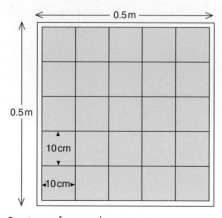

Sections of a quadrat.

A quadrat must always be positioned randomly.

Sampling using a quadrat works best if:

- the quadrat is placed **randomly**

- a **reasonable number of samples** is taken, so any 'odd' results will be 'evened out' when averages are taken

- the plants being investigated are reasonably **evenly spread** throughout the area.

You could also place a quadrat at regular intervals **along a line** to see how the habitat changes. This is called a **transect**.

Quadrats can also be used to investigate the numbers or distribution of **animals** in a habitat, as long as they are evenly distributed and not constantly moving around the area.

QUESTIONS

Q1 A pupil wanted to estimate the number of dandelions in a field. She used a large quadrat that was $1m^2$ and the field was $200m^2$. She used the quadrat 10 times and counted a total of 25 dandelions. Estimate the number of dandelions in the field.

Q2 Why is it important that quadrats are placed randomly?

Q3 What is an ecosystem?

Answers are on page 162.

More questions on the CD ROM

FEEDING RELATIONSHIPS

FOOD CHAINS

Food chains show how living things get their food. They also show how they get their **energy**. This is why they are sometimes written to include the Sun.

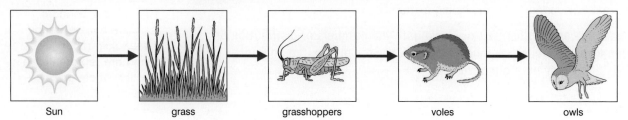

| Sun | grass | grasshoppers | voles | owls |

An example of a food chain.

Food chains can be written going up or down a page, or even from right to left. All are correct, as long as the arrows always point **towards** the living thing that is taking in the food or energy.

Stages of a food chain

Producers are the green plants (such as grass). They make their own food by **photosynthesis**, using energy from the Sun. **Primary consumers** (such as grasshoppers) are animals that **eat plants** or parts of plants, such as fruit. They are also called **herbivores**. **Secondary consumers** (such as voles) eat other animals. They may be called **carnivores** or **predators**. **Tertiary consumers** (such as owls) are animals that eat some secondary consumers. They are also called carnivores or predators. The animals hunted and eaten by predators are called **prey**. Animals that eat both plants and animals are called **omnivores**.

The different stages of a food chain are sometimes called **trophic levels** (trophic means 'feeding'). So, for example, producers make up the first trophic level, primary consumers make up the second trophic level and so on.

Most food chains are not very long. They usually end with a secondary consumer or a tertiary consumer, but occasionally there is an animal that feeds on tertiary consumers. This would be called a **quaternary consumer**.

Eventually all the organisms involved in the food chain will die and become food for decomposers, organisms such as bacteria and fungi that break down dead plants and animals.

FOOD WEBS

Food webs are different food chains joined together. It would be unusual to find a food chain that was not part of a larger food web. Here is part of a food web:

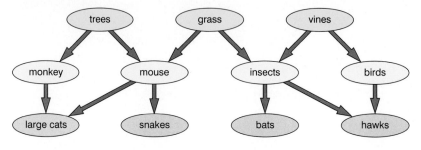

Food webs show how different animals feed, and they can help us see what might happen if the food web is disturbed in some way.

For example, what might happen if there was a disease that killed many, if not all, the monkeys? From the food web above you can see that the cats would have to eat more of the other animals, which might result in fewer mice. On the other hand, there would be more trees for the mice to eat, which might mean there are more mice.

It is not possible to say for sure what would happen to all the organisms in a food web because there are so many living things involved.

PYRAMIDS OF NUMBER, BIOMASS AND ENERGY

Food chains usually begin with organisms that are numerous and pass through trophic levels of decreasing numbers until they reach the top predators. For example many green plants are eaten by a smaller number of herbivores, like deer, which then feed only a few tigers.

Pyramids can be drawn to show either organisms from a single food chain or the trophic levels in a food web. If they show trophic levels, **each stage of the pyramid is labelled** by role, for example, producers or primary consumers.

Pyramids of numbers show the **relative numbers** of each type of living thing in a food chain or web by trophic level.

Occasionally a lesser number of large producers could be consumed by many small consumers; in this case the pyramid may be inverted.

Pyramids of biomass show the dry mass of living material at each level. Pyramids of biomass are almost **never** inverted.

But pyramids of biomass produce problems of their own. The mass of the tree is actually a measure of the biomass accumulated over many years. This is often called the standing crop. The insects living off it may have been produced and consumed in a matter of days and so do not accumulate biomass in the same way. This produces the correct shape for the pyramid but creates a different problem.

The growth of plankton in an area of sea was measured over a few days and a pyramid of biomass created (see below right). Again the pyramid is inverted. This is due to 'under sampling' of the algae supporting the food web caused by the relatively short life span of the algae compared with the longer-lived herbivorous organisms. Unlike the tree they are not producing a significant standing crop so do not provide a significant base layer for the ecosystem. To solve this problem ecologists look not at the biomass but at the energy transferred between trophic levels.

Pyramids of energy give a much better view of the energy flow through the ecosystem. They always show the typical pyramid shape and take account of total energy passing through the system rather than the amounts stored at each level as biomass during a particular sampling period. Uniquely, pyramids of energy take into account the energy transferred in unit time whereas the pyramids of number and biomass take no account of the time over which materials have been accumulated and transformed.

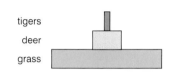

A pyramid of numbers

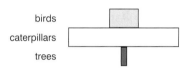

An inverted pyramid of numbers

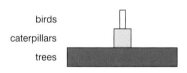

A pyramid of biomass

A pyramid of numbers

A pyramid of biomass

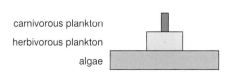

A pyramid of energy

ENERGY FLOW

The arrows in food chains and webs show the **transfer of energy**. Not all the energy that enters an animal or plant is available to the next trophic level. Only energy that has resulted in an organism's growth will be available to the animal that eats it. For example, cows feeding on grass in a field:

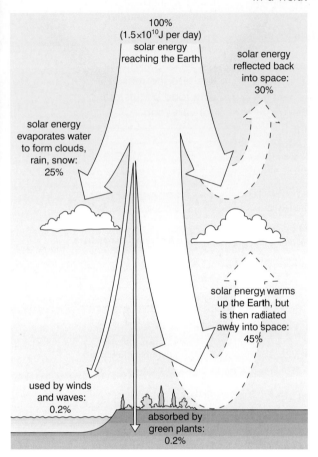

100%
(1.5×10^{10}J per day)
solar energy reaching the Earth

solar energy reflected back into space: 30%

solar energy evaporates water to form clouds, rain, snow: 25%

solar energy warms up the Earth, but is then radiated away into space: 45%

used by winds and waves: 0.2%

absorbed by green plants: 0.2%

Energy flow in plants.

Sun → grass → cow

Only a **small proportion** of the energy in the sunlight falling on a field is used by the grass in photosynthesis:

- some energy may be **absorbed** or **reflected** by **clouds** or **dust** in the air

- some energy may be absorbed or reflected by **trees** or **other plants**

- some energy may **miss** the grass and hit the ground

- some energy will be reflected by the **grass** (grass reflects the green part of the spectrum and absorbs the red and blue wavelengths)

- some energy will enter the grass but will **pass through** the leaves.

The remainder of the energy can be used in photosynthesis. Some of the food made by the grass will be used for respiration to provide the grass's energy requirements, but some will be used for growth and will be available for a future consumer.

However, not all the energy in the grass will be available to the cows:

- some grass may be eaten by **other animals** (the farmer would probably call these pests)

- the cows will **not eat all** of the grass (for example the roots will be left).

Of the energy available in the grass the cows do **ingest** (eat), they will use only a small proportion for growth. The diagram on the page opposite shows what happens to the energy in an animal's food.

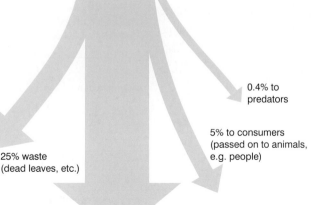

100% radiation energy absorbed by plants

0.4% to predators

5% to consumers (passed on to animals, e.g. people)

25% waste (dead leaves, etc.)

70% stored (in wood, etc.)

How animals lose energy
Energy is lost from animals in two main ways:

1 **egestion and excretion** – the removal from the body, in faeces, of material that may contain energy but has not been digested, and the loss of urea and other compounds in urine and sweat

2 **respiration** – the release of energy from food is necessary for all the processes that go on in living things, such as movement, most of this energy is eventually lost as heat.

Because **energy is lost** from the chain **at each stage** you almost always get a pyramid shape with a pyramid of biomass.

The decreasing amounts of energy that can be transferred from one trophic level to another can also be thought of in terms of a pyramid.

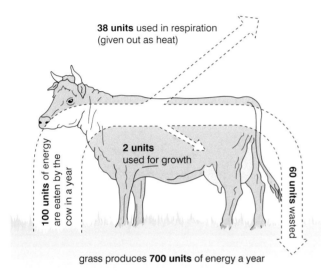

38 units used in respiration (given out as heat)

The energy flow in a young cow.

100 units of energy are eaten by the cow in a year

2 units used for growth

60 units wasted

grass produces **700 units** of energy a year

QUESTIONS

Q1 Look at this food chain in a garden:
rose bushes → aphids → ladybirds
a Draw and label a pyramid of numbers for this food chain.
b Draw and label a pyramid of biomass for this food chain.

Q2 Why are there usually not more than five stages in a food chain?

Q3 What are the two main ways in which animals in a food chain lose energy?

Answers are on page 162.

More questions on the CD ROM

CYCLES WITHIN ECOSYSTEMS

THE WATER CYCLE

As you know water, H_2O, is essential to life processes. Fortunately the world's water does not get used up; it is constantly recycled.

Most of the world's water is in the oceans. Some evaporates into the atmosphere. Water vapour is transported in the atmosphere until it condenses into clouds and eventually falls as precipitation. Some will return straight to the ocean, but some falls on land. Much of this water will drain into rivers and return to the oceans. Some will be used by plants and animals.

Plants use water in transport and photosynthesis; animals use water for transport, to excrete substances and to regulate temperature through sweating. Plants obtain water through their roots. Animals obtain water from eating plants and other animals, as well as drinking. Both animals and plants give off water as a by-product of respiration.

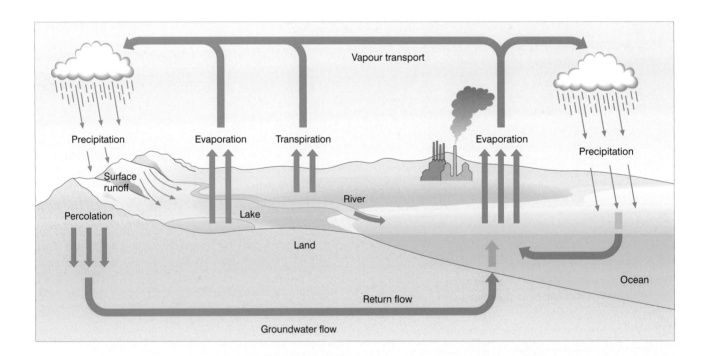

THE CARBON CYCLE

Plants take in carbon dioxide because they need the **carbon** (and oxygen) to use in photosynthesis to make carbohydrates and then other substances such as protein.

When animals eat plants they use some of the carbon-containing compounds to grow and some to release energy by respiration.

As a waste product of respiration, animals breathe out carbon as carbon dioxide, which is then available for plants to use. (Don't forget that plants also respire producing carbon dioxide.)

Carbon dioxide is also released when animal and plant remains decay (**decomposition**) and when wood, peat or fossil fuels are burnt (**combustion**).

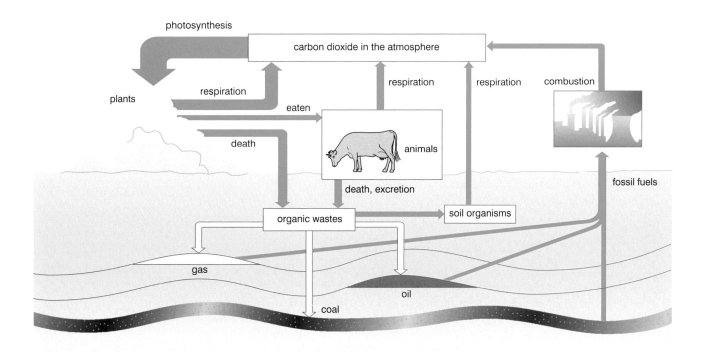

THE NITROGEN CYCLE

Living things need **nitrogen** to make proteins, which are needed, for example, to make new cells for growth.

Air is 79% nitrogen gas (N_2), but nitrogen gas is very unreactive and cannot be used by plants or animals. Instead plants use nitrogen in the form of **nitrates (NO_3^- ions)**.

The process of getting nitrogen into this useful form is called **nitrogen fixation**.

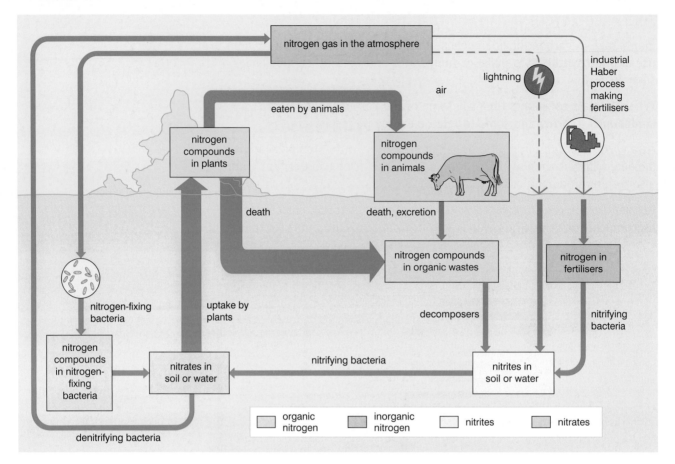

Animals get nitrogen when they take in protein by eating meat or plant material.

Nitrogen-fixing bacteria take nitrogen from the air (don't forget there is air in soil) to form nitrogen-containing compounds such as nitrates. Some of these bacteria are free-living in the soil but some live in swellings, called root nodules, in the roots of leguminous plants, e.g. beans, peas and clover.

Nitrifying bacteria convert ammonia from the decayed remains and waste of animals and plants into nitrates.

Denitrifying bacteria convert nitrates back into nitrogen.

QUESTIONS

Q1 **a** In the carbon cycle, which main process removes carbon dioxide from the atmosphere?
b How is carbon dioxide put back into the atmosphere?

Q2 Nitrogen-fixing bacteria cannot live in waterlogged soil but denitrifying bacteria can, which is why this kind of soil is low in nitrates. Some plants that live in these conditions are carnivorous, trapping and digesting insects. Suggest why you often find carnivorous plants in bogs.

Q3 What is the difference between nitrifying and denitrifying bacteria?

More questions on the CD ROM

Answers are on page 162.

HUMAN INFLUENCES ON THE ENVIRONMENT

THE GREENHOUSE EFFECT

Water vapour, carbon carbon dioxide, nitrous oxide, methane and CFCs all act as **greenhouse gases**. Water vapour is present due to many natural processes but the levels of these other gases in the atmosphere are increasing due to the burning of fossil fuels, pollution from farm animals and the use of CFCs in aerosols and refrigerators.

Short-wave radiation from the Sun warms the ground and the warm Earth gives off heat as long-wave radiation. Much of this radiation is stopped from escaping from the Earth by the greenhouse gases. This is known as the **greenhouse effect**.

The greenhouse effect is responsible for keeping the Earth warmer than it otherwise would be. The greenhouse effect is normal, and important for life on Earth. However, it is thought that increasing levels of greenhouse gases are trapping more heat than is normal, and the Earth is warming up. This is known as **global warming**. If global warming continues the Earth's climate may change and sea levels rise as polar ice melts.

The temperature of the Earth is gradually increasing, but we do not know for certain if the greenhouse effect is responsible. It may be that the observed rise in recent global temperatures is part of a natural cycle: there have been ice ages and intermediate warm periods before. Many people are concerned that it is not part of a cycle and say we should act now to reduce emissions of greenhouse gases.

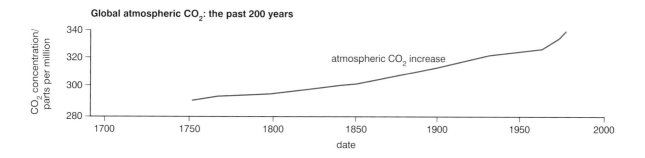

Global atmospheric CO_2: the past 200 years

atmospheric CO_2 increase

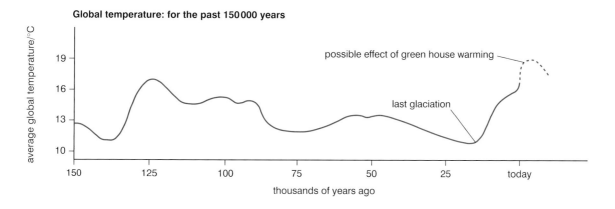

Global temperature: for the past 150 000 years

possible effect of green house warming

last glaciation

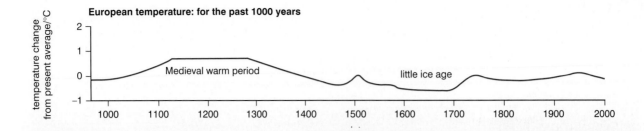

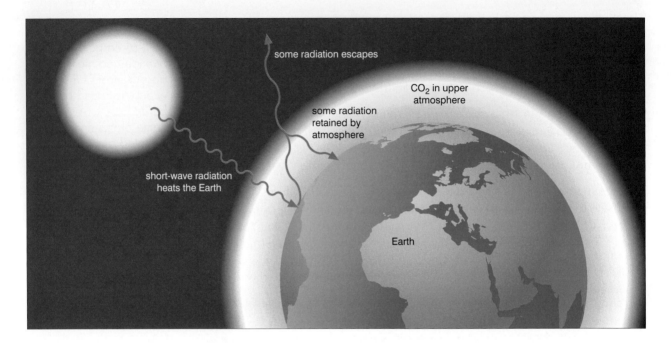

ACID RAIN

Burning fossil fuels gives off many gases, including **sulphur dioxide** and various **nitrogen oxides**.

Sulphur dioxide combines with water to form **sulphuric acid**. Nitrogen oxide combines with water to form **nitric acid**. These substances can make the rain acidic (**acid rain**).

Acid rain **harms plants** that take in the acidic water **and animals** that live in affected rivers and lakes. Acid rain washes ions, such as calcium and magnesium, out of the soil, **depleting the minerals available to plants**. It also washes **aluminium compounds**, which are poisonous to fish, out of the soil and into rivers and lakes.

Reducing emissions of the gases causing acid rain is expensive, and part of the problem is that the acid rain usually falls a long way from the places where the gases were given off.

Fitting **catalytic converters** stops the emission of these gases from cars.

Sulphur impurities caused from burning fuels can be reduced by:

- treating fuels before burning

- modifying chimneys of power stations by adding acid gas scrubbers, which neutralise the acid.

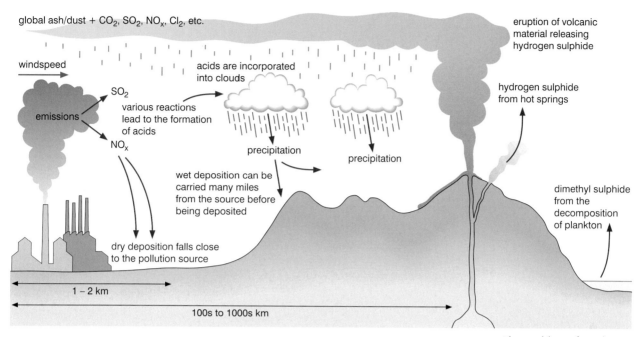

global ash/dust + CO_2, SO_2, NO_x, Cl_2, etc.

eruption of volcanic material releasing hydrogen sulphide

windspeed

acids are incorporated into clouds

SO_2

various reactions lead to the formation of acids

emissions

NO_x

precipitation

precipitation

hydrogen sulphide from hot springs

wet deposition can be carried many miles from the source before being deposited

dry deposition falls close to the pollution source

dimethyl sulphide from the decomposition of plankton

1 – 2 km

100s to 1000s km

The problem of acid rain.

CARBON MONOXIDE

Carbon monoxide is a colourless, odourless gas. It is formed when substances containing carbon are burned with an insufficient supply of air. The use of fuels such as petrol, gas, coal and wood generate emissions of carbon monoxide. Motor vehicles engines are the main source of carbon monoxide pollution in urban areas; car exhaust emissions contain carbon monoxide.

Carbon monoxide can have serious health impacts on humans and animals. When inhaled, the carbon monoxide bonds to the haemoglobin in the blood to produce carboxyhaemoglobin. The oxygen-carrying capacity of the red blood cells and the supply of oxygen to tissues and organs are reduced. The effects on the heart and brain are particularly significant and an increase in carbon monoxide can be a serious problem for people with cardiovascular disease. The formation of carboxyhaemoglobin is reversible when the person is no longer exposed to carbon monoxide.

SEWAGE POLLUTION

With the rapid increase in the world's population in recent years the problem of sewage disposal is growing. Contamination of water courses and of the sea with sewage can lead to many problems.

A small amount of sewage in a large area does not cause great problems and can in fact provide nutrients. Too great a concentration, however, can lead to excessive growth of plants in rivers and lakes, and coastal waters, especially **algae**. Plants growing over the surface of the water makes the water murky and blocks much of the light, and plants under the surface die and decay. The bacteria that cause the decay use up the oxygen in the water, so fish and other water animals die. This whole process is called **eutrophication**. Eutrophication can also be caused by the leaching of excessive fertiliser applied to farmland.

This river is blocked with algae because of excess nitrates washed in from nearby fields.

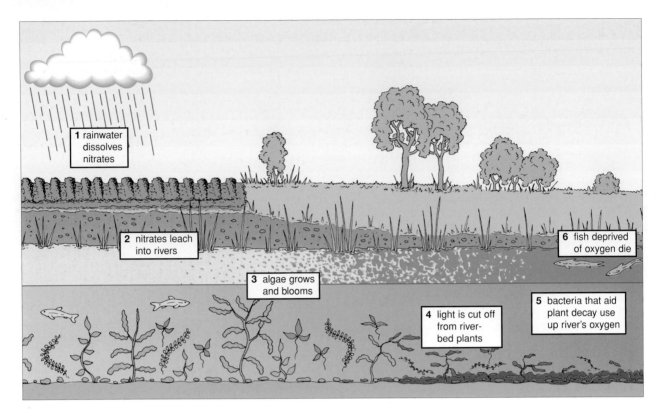

The process of eutrophication.

1 rainwater dissolves nitrates

2 nitrates leach into rivers

3 algae grows and blooms

4 light is cut off from river-bed plants

5 bacteria that aid plant decay use up river's oxygen

6 fish deprived of oxygen die

Sewage pollution contamination of drinking water, seafood or bathing water is also to blame for outbreaks of infectious gastrointestinal disease such as cholera.

DEFORESTATION

Deforestation is the permanent destruction of indigenous forests and woodlands. Large areas of rainforest are being cut down for their wood and to create farming or grazing land. Forests act as a major carbon store because carbon dioxide is taken up from the atmosphere during photosynthesis and used to produce the chemical compounds that make up the tree. When forests are cleared, and the trees are either burnt or rot, this carbon is released as carbon dioxide. This upsets the balance of atmospheric oxygen and carbon dioxide. Carbon dioxide is a major contributor to the greenhouse effect.

An example of a habitat destroyed by human actions.

Deforestation also has an effect on the water cycle. Trees draw ground water up through their roots and release it into the atmosphere by transpiration. As forest trees are removed the amount of water that can be held in an area decreases with possible effects on the local climate.

Removing the protective cover of vegetation from the soil can also result in soil being eroded. It is washed away by rain into streams and rivers where it may cause silting up of water courses.

All these effects will change the ecosystem of an area and may result in the loss of species and a decrease in biodiversity.

OVERFISHING AND OVERGRAZING

The increase in world population and the subsequent increase in demand for food is putting ever greater demands on our food production industry. Overfishing and overgrazing are two possible consequences of this.

Overfishing is said to have occurred when the population of one or more species of fish is reduced below a sustainable level as the result of fishing activities. Ultimately this could lead to the destruction of populations of fish within an area and a change in the local ecosystem. To prevent overfishing, agreement needs to be made amongst all those involved in the fishing industry to limit catches to levels that will allow populations to survive.

Overgrazing can be caused by having too many grazing animals on an area or by poor grazing management. As plant leaves are eaten, less area is left in which photosynthesis can occur, and plant growth is therefore reduced. Plants become weakened and have reduced root length. Smaller roots make the plants more susceptible to drought and to competition from other species. It can also allow soil erosion to occur. Once again these effects can lead to an alteration in the ecosystem.

QUESTIONS

Q1 What is the difference between the greenhouse effect and global warming?

Q2 Acid rain can be reduced by passing waste gases through lime to remove sulphur dioxide. Why do all factories not automatically do this?

Q3 What is eutrophication and what can it be caused by?

More questions on the CD ROM

Answers are on page 162.

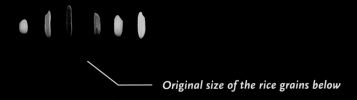

Original size of the rice grains below

wild rice

natural rice

Italian risotto rice

A golden future?

Traditionally, farmers have used selective breeding to improve their crops and farm animals, by picking the best ones to breed from. The results of this have been varieties and breeds that are ideally suited to the community's particular needs.

Genetic engineering may provide a new strategy. By artificially transferring genes from one species to another, scientists can develop transgenic crops and trees that are resistant to disease or insecticides and that have greater yields. However, some of the early genetically modified crops, such as maize, have generated considerable controversy, and there has been widespread debate about the possible risks of transferring genes between organisms.

There are many potential benefits, though. 'Golden rice', for instance, is a genetically modified rice. It is yellow because it carries an extra gene that produces beta-carotene, which the body converts into vitamin A. Vitamin A deficiency is common in malnourished people and leads to blindness and other diseases. By developing golden rice, scientists hope to help reduce these diseases.

Chapter 5

USE OF BIOLOGICAL RESOURCES

partly boiled (parboiled) rice

milk rice

Golden rice

FOOD PRODUCTION

Crop plants

PROTECTED CULTIVATION

If plants are grown in greenhouses or polythene tunnels they can be protected from the environment. Temperature, levels of water, fertiliser and even carbon dioxide can be carefully controlled to ensure maximum yields. Increasing the availability of all of these factors that are normally found in outdoor conditions will tend to increase growth.

The level of carbon dioxide normally present in the outside air will allow plants to grow well but increasing the level of carbon dioxide increases the rate of photosynthesis and thus the rate of growth. Increasing the temperature will tend to increase the rate of metabolic reactions although temperatures that are too high are damaging. The increased growth due to carbon dioxide supplementation and warmth creates a greater demand for nutrients and water. Protection also allows crops to be produced in areas that would be too cold for them or at times that are outside their normal growing season.

Polytunnels in Tibet are now supplying green vegetables that previously could not be grown in the cold mountainous regions.

Crop grown in greenhouse	No added Carbon dioxide	Carbon dioxide added
Fresh weight of 10 lettuce plants in kg	0.9	2.5
Fresh weight of saleable tomato fruits in kg	4.4	6.4

FERTILISERS

Plants need water and light for photosynthesis but need other substances in order to grow well. These are called mineral nutrients and come from the soil. Faeces (manure) contain large supplies of one of the most valuable nutrients, nitrogen.

Plants use nitrogen to make proteins, nucleic acids and chlorophyll. If the soil does not contain enough nitrogen the plants do not grow well. Their leaves are often yellowish in colour.

Fertilisers, like manure, also contain a range of other chemicals that help to improve the soil. Because manure comes from a living source it is called an organic fertiliser. Artificial fertilisers are made in chemical factories and are applied as a powder. These are called inorganic fertilisers and supply mineral salts.

MINERALS

The table shows the main mineral nutrients needed for healthy growth. Mineral nutrients are absorbed into the plant through the roots as simple salts like potassium phosphate or ammonium sulphate. Fertiliser packets often show how much of the key elements are present in the mixture. This allows a gardener or farmer to work out how much to add to the soil. It is important to get the dose right:

Plant with nitrogen deficiency

• Too little fertiliser and the plants will not grow well.

• Too much fertiliser can harm plant growth and high levels of nitrogen in the soil can damage nearby rivers and lakes. Fertiliser is also expensive, so you don't want to waste it.

Mineral nutrient	Use in plant	Effects of deficiency
Nitrogen	Proteins, nucleic acids, chlorophyll	Reduced growth and yellowish leaves
Potassium	Essential for some enzyme reactions	Poor growth, older leaves become mottled
Phosphorus	Nucleic acids and a range of other substances including ATP	Poor root growth

Plant with phosphorous deficiency

PESTICIDES

Plants do not provide food just for humans. A wide range of other animals and insects will eat crop plants if they are not protected. These animals are called pests and farmers use pesticides to kill them. Pesticides are poisons but chemists have tried to ensure that they only poison the pests, not the crop plants or the consumers of the food.

Pesticides are used in very low concentrations, sometimes so low that they cannot be detected on the original plants. If an organism eats the plant it will absorb the pesticide and can store it in its body. If it eats 20 plants, will it collect 20 times the pesticide? If another animal eats this one, will it take in 20 times the dose of pesticide it would get from the plant? If it eats 20 animals will it absorb 20 times 20?

Research done in the 1950s and 1960s showed how the levels of a pesticide called DDT changed in the environment. Low levels of DDT were sprayed onto a lake in the USA to kill mosquitoes. This was a success in that it got rid of the mosquitoes, but green plants absorbed some of the DDT. These plants were eaten by small animals, which in turn were eaten by fish who were eaten by small birds and so on up to the large predatory birds like ospreys. At every step in the chain the levels of DDT detected in the organism rose. This increase in concentration is called **bioaccumulation**.

By the 1970s the levels of DDT in large birds was so high that populations were beginning to crash. A tiny amount of DDT in the water threatened to make some birds extinct and DDT was banned. Even after 30 years the number of predatory birds is still quite low and the recovery will take many more years. More worryingly, even birds many kilometres away from the original sprayed sites showed dangerously high levels of DDT.

BIOLOGICAL CONTROL

An alternative approach to pesticides is to use biological control systems. Pests can be food for other creatures and if these creatures are introduced into a field they will destroy the pests and so protect the crops.

The prickly pear cactus was introduced to Australia by accident. It grew so rapidly that at one point it covered 12 million hectares of grazing land. The moth Cactoblastis produces larvae that damage the prickly pear. Introducing the moth into prickly-pear-infested areas reduced the problem dramatically in only a few years. The 13th century Chinese used to place ants on citrus plants to prevent infestations of aphids.

	Advantages	Disadvantages
Pesticides	Initially very effective Easy to apply Can be used with almost all crops	Pests can develop resistance to pesticides Bioaccumulation can damage other living things Expensive
Biological control systems	Not 100 per cent effective No poisons involved so no harm to wildlife or humans	Can be difficult to apply Not suitable for all crops

Microorganisms

As technology advances, we are turning our attention towards the effective use of different organisms.

We use the properties and processes of some microorganisms to produce types of food and drink:

- bread – a yeast (fungus) and sugar mixture is added to flour to form a dough, and the **respiration** of yeast produces carbon dioxide, which raises the dough

- cheese – a culture of bacteria is added to warm milk and the resulting curds are separated from the liquid whey, more bacteria and special moulds are added to the curds and the cheese slowly ripens, with other moulds sometimes added to give flavour and colour to the cheese

- vinegar – a mixture of beer, wine or ethanol and nutrients is poured over wood shavings coated with a bacteria *Acetobacter*, and this bacteria **converts** ethanol into vinegar

- soy sauce – cooked soya beans and roasted wheat are fermented, filtered and then pasteurised

- **single-cell protein (SCP)**, also called **mycoprotein** – this is a fungus that is mixed with carbohydrate and kept in warm conditions so that it grows rapidly, then the fungus is separated and dried.

THE BREWING OF BEER

The production of alcohol is another process that utilises yeast. The anaerobic respiration of yeast produces ethanol, the basis of alcoholic drinks, and carbon dioxide which can give the drink a sparkling or frothy quality.

glucose → alcohol + carbon dioxide + water

In beer-brewing the starch breaks down into a sugar solution inside the germinating barley grains. This is called the malting stage. The sugar solution is then drained off and fermented with the yeast. The flavour of the beer is developed by adding hops to the mixture.

EXPERIMENT TO INVESTIGATE YEASTS AND ANAEROBIC RESPIRATION

Yeasts carry out anaerobic respiration to produce carbon dioxide and ethanol. This simple experiment investigates the effect of ethanol on yeast respiration by monitoring the amount of carbon dioxide evolved.

You will need:

- 5 boiling tubes
- 5 small test tubes
- Water bath
- Boiling tube stand
- 10ml syringe
- Yeast solution
- Sucrose solution
- 50 per cent ethanol in water solution
- Olive oil

Safety note:
Alcohol is flammable and should never be used near a naked flame.

1 Prepare a reaction tube by submerging both a boiling tube and a small test tube in water so that all the air comes out of both. While they are still underwater push the small test tube into the boiling tube with its top pointing to the bottom of the boiling tube. Remove the tubes from the water and pour out water until the bottom of the test tube (pointing upwards) is just submerged. Repeat this process so that you have 5 reaction tubes. Place these in a stand and label each one with a number from 1 to 5.

2 Mix 10ml of yeast solution with 15ml of sucrose solution.

3 Add 5ml of this solution to tubes 1 to 5.

4 Add 1ml of the ethanol in water solution to tube 1, 2ml to tube 2, 3ml to tube 3, 4 ml to tube 4.

5 Float a layer of olive oil over the surface of the yeast mixture in the boiling tubes. This ensures anaerobic conditions in the yeast culture.

6 Leave the tubes in a water bath at 35°C for 30 minutes or overnight if no water bath is available.

7 To collect results measure the height of the small test tube showing above the level of the yeast and sugar solution.

1 Completely submerge both tubes so that all the air comes out.

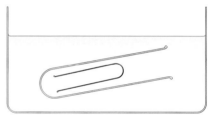

2 Push the test tube inside the boiling tube.

3 Pour off the excess water to leave the test tube just submerged.

Sample results

Tube	Alcohol added	Height of small tube
1	1	4
2	2	3
3	3	1
4	4	0
5	0	6

Data response questions

1 What effect does alcohol have on the rate of respiration in yeasts?

2 How could you modify this experiment to look at the effect of temperature on alcoholic inhibition of yeast respiration?

Answers are on page 125.

Discussion

The yeast produces carbon dioxide, which collects in the small tube making it float above the surface of the liquid in the boiling tube. The volume of gas produced, indicated by the height of the tube, is a measure of the activity of the yeast. This system provides an easy way to investigate the growth of yeast in a range of conditions. The sample results here show that yeast is poisoned by ethanol when the concentration rises above a certain point. This explains why the brewing industry has to resort to distillation to produce drinks with an alcohol content of above about 15 per cent ethanol. The system can also be used to investigate the effect of temperature on the rate of respiration by using tubes containing yeast maintained at a range of different temperatures. The height of the small tubes above the water level after a given length of time will then provide a measure of the rate of the reaction.

THE PRODUCTION OF YOGHURT

Milk is pasteurised to kill any unwanted bacteria, cultures of *Lactobacillus* bacteria are then added and the mixture is maintained at 46°C. The bacteria feed on the milk and grow, releasing lactic acid, which has a preservative effect. The acid pH causes the milk protein to coagulate.

USING MICROORGANISMS ON A LARGE SCALE

Microorganisms can be used to make chemicals on a **large scale**. For example, by growing the fungus *Penicillium* in a **fermenter** the antibiotic penicillin can be made in large quantities. The fungus is fed glucose and ammonia, and the fermenter is kept at 25°C.

The enzymes that help to speed up the process of fermentation have an optimum temperature. Most enzymes are denatured above 60°C and work very slowly at low temperatures.

A fermenter is filled with a small amount of the desired microorganism (or microbe), for example yeast, and a **growth medium**. The most suitable conditions for growth are created, including the correct pH.

Heat: the reactions inside the fermenter release heat. Water passes through a cooling jacket to make sure the temperature does not rise too high. If the temperature gets too high the enzymes would be denatured.

Oxygen: sterile air is pumped in at the bottom of the fermenter. Stirrers rotate the inside of the fermenter to make sure oxygen is distributed through the mixture so that aerobic respiration can take place.

A* EXTRA

- Fuels can be made from natural products by fermentation. Biogas (mainly methane) can be produced by anaerobic fermentation of plant products or waste materials. Many different microorganisms are used in the breakdown of materials for the production of biogas.

Sterile conditions: pumping super-heated steam through the fermenter before using it destroys any unwanted microorganisms.

After fermentation, the products are taken from a tap at the bottom of the fermenter.

The products can then be purified, separated, packaged and marketed.

Fish farming

Fish is an excellent low fat, high protein food and is becoming more popular every year. To supply this growing market suppliers are building **fish farms** where they can make sure the fish are kept in optimum conditions for growth. An open fish farm is little more than a large pond or lake where fish are kept. The site needs to be carefully selected to ensure that a water supply of adequate quality is available. Water must be free of fish diseases and parasites, nuisance fish, predators, silt, pesticides, chlorine, and other chemicals that are harmful to fish life. Water from springs or wells is best. Carefully controlled amounts of animal manure are added to encourage growth of pondweeds. The fish feed on these weeds and can be netted when they are big enough to eat, which is typically between four and six years.

On some fish farms the fish are kept in an enclosed system. Food is added and the fish are harvested when they have reached a suitable size. To stock the farm, eggs and sperm are removed from adult fish and then mixed in the laboratory. The eggs are hatched in tanks of gently flowing water and when the young fish are a suitable size they are added to the tanks. Since the fish's breeding is controlled it is possible to select for the best fish rather like farmers used to choose the best cow to breed from.

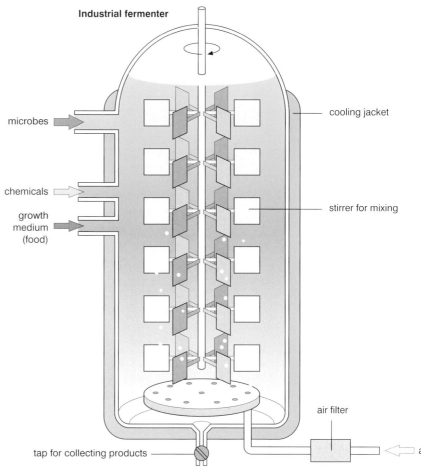

Industrial fermenter

- cooling jacket
- microbes
- chemicals
- growth medium (food)
- stirrer for mixing
- air filter
- tap for collecting products
- air

A* EXTRA

- Make sure you understand and can explain the design of an industrial fermenter.

Traditional methods of fishing can no longer meet the growing demand for fish.

As the cages are well stocked with fish, infection is more likely. The farmer often adds pesticides to the fish food to protect the stock from pests. These pesticides can leak out into the environment beyond the cages. Farmed fish typically has ten times the level of the dangerous pollutant PCB found in wild fish.

Fish produce wastes, which must be removed. These are typically washed away in ocean systems but fall to the bottom of the pond in enclosed systems. This means the ponds have to be drained, cleaned and restocked roughly every six years.

Fish are very efficient convertors of input energy into meat. They do not keep their bodies above environmental temperature like mammals so they do not waste food energy doing this. In 2002 the total amount of protein produced by fish exceeded that of beef cattle on a global scale. About 27 per cent of the global fish protein was produced by farmed fish, up from just under 4 per cent in 1970.

Fish farmers maximise production by:
- stocking fish at high densities (but note that overstocking may lead to problems of intraspecific predation, when the fish prey on each other)
- supplying adequate, high quality food
- choosing the best fish to breed from
- protecting against pests with chemical pesticides
- taking steps to minimise risk of disease, e.g. infectious salmon anaemia
- protection from predators (mammals, birds, reptiles, other species of fish)
- removing waste products.

QUESTIONS

Q1 Jayne is making yoghurt. The process involves three stages:
A milk is pasteurised
B the bacteria *Lactobacillus* is added to milk and cultured
C lactic acid is released into the milk.
a Explain why the milk is pasteurised.
b Suggest why only a small amount of *Lactobacillus* is added to the milk.
c Jayne heated the mixture to 80°C. Explain why the mixture did not turn into yoghurt.

Q2 Industrial fermenters are filled with nutrients and a small amount of a microbe, such as bacteria. This process is used to make useful chemicals on a large scale.
a Suggest why only a small amount of microbe needs to be used.
b Explain why microbes such as bacteria are suitable for use in industrial fermenters.
c Suggest two useful chemicals that can be produced using industrial fermenters.

Q3 How can increasing the concentration of carbon dioxide in a polytunnel improve the yield of a plant crop?

Q4 Name three things the presence of which in water could be harmful to farmed fish.

More questions on the CD ROM

Answers are on page 163.

SELECTIVE BREEDING

Plants

Plants have long been selectively bred for improved yield and disease resistance. In wheat there has been a change from longer-stemmed plants with few grains to shorter-stemmed plants in which more of the sugar produced by photosynthesis is devoted to seed production. Primitive wheat plants had long stems because they were used for straw to feed cattle and a range of other purposes. As the need for straw reduced so the features selected by farmers changed.

Wheat has been bred to:
• reduce growth of non-edible parts
• increase yield
• increase disease resistance
• improve ability to survive adverse climates
• improve food quality (increase the amount of protein in the seed).

Rice is a staple food for billions of people in the world and has been the subject of extensive modern scientific cross-breeding. New breeds of rice called High Yielding Varieties or HYVs were produced by the International Rice Research Institute in the Philippines in the 1970s. Cross-breeding plants involves taking pollen from one plant and adding it to the seed-producing parts of other plants. In this way useful characteristics could be built up in the new seeds.

An HYV of rice produced twice as much grain as the old variety. New breeding programs produced even better varieties. Rice plants from around the world were crossed in breeding experiments to produce the so-called 'miracle rices'. But the plants required extra fertiliser and plenty of water to produce the high yields. The modern seeds were also very expensive. If the conditions were not perfect the new HYVs could sometimes do worse than the traditional varieties and in some countries the productivity actually went down. Scientists began to appreciate how important the environment was to the way the genes worked. The old-fashioned varieties had evolved over thousands of years to cope with bad conditions.

Old-fashioned varieties of rice have evolved to survive in the particular conditions in which they grow.

Animals

Farmers have controlled the breeding of their animals and plants since agriculture was invented over 5,000 years ago. By selecting animals that match the farmers' needs and breeding only from these, farmers have created domesticated animals that are dramatically different from their wild ancestors. Even within one species, breeds can be selected for particular purposes so one breed of cow is good for meat production while another is chosen for milk yields.

The original cow was larger and more difficult to manage than modern breeds. It grew more slowly and produced less milk. Over thousands of years farmers have bred for:
- increased growth
- increased milk production
- docility
- resistance to disease.

Different breeds have different advantages, often linked to the conditions where they are farmed or the product (milk or meat) required.

Cows have long been bred according to the particular requirements of the farmer and the environment.

Cattle breed	Original home	Features
N'dama	West Africa	Resistant to tsetse fly which spreads the cattle disease trypanosomoniasis, which kills other breeds. Copes well with hot dry climates.
Holstein	Netherlands	Excellent milk producer. These are now the most common dairy cows in the world.
Hereford	England	Excellent meat production, very adaptable, particularly for cooler climates.
Yak	Tibet	A relative of the cow, the yak provides milk and meat in very cold regions, it is also used as a beast of burden.

QUESTIONS

Q1 Suggest three qualities you might want to select for in a food plant.

Q2 A farmer wants to produce sheep with finer wool. How could this be done by selective breeding?

More questions on the CD ROM

Answers are on page 163.

GENETIC MODIFICATION

The structure of DNA

The blueprint for building an organism, bacterium, plant or animal is encoded in the structure of the chemical deoxyribonucleic acid or DNA.

Each DNA molecule is made up of two strands twisting around each other in what is famously known as the 'double helix'.

Each strand is composed of millions of **nucleotides**, each consisting of a **phosphate molecule**, a deoxyribose sugar molecule and a **base**. There are four possible different bases in DNA: adenine (A), thymine (T), cytosine (C) and guanine (G).

The bases are arranged on the inside of the helix and links are formed between the bases on each strand. Adenine must link to thymine and guanine to cytosine. It is the sequence of bases that forms the genetic code.

A **restriction enzyme** is an enzyme that cuts DNA. The enzyme cuts through the phosphate backbones of the double helix without damaging the bases. Different enzymes known as **ligases** can be used to join fragments of DNA together. These techniques can be used in genetic modification.

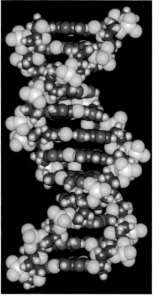

The 'double helix' structure of DNA

Steps involved in genetic modification

1 **Find** the part of the DNA that contains the gene you want.

2 **Remove the gene** using restriction enzymes to cut the DNA either side of the gene.

3 **Insert the gene** into the genetic material of the organism you want to change using ligase enzymes.

Step 3 may be done directly but it often involves using **vectors**. Vectors may be viruses or plasmids. A plasmid is a circular unit of DNA that replicates within a cell, usually a bacterium, independently of the chromosomal DNA. The gene is first inserted in the vectors, which then transfer the gene to the desired host when they infect it.

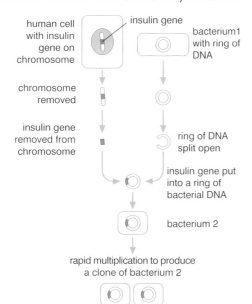

The process of genetic modification used for insulin production.

human cell with insulin gene on chromosome

insulin gene

bacterium1 with ring of DNA

chromosome removed

insulin gene removed from chromosome

ring of DNA split open

insulin gene put into a ring of bacterial DNA

bacterium 2

rapid multiplication to produce a clone of bacterium 2

Insertion of a genetically modified plasmid into bacteria followed by the culture of the bacteria in a fermenter can allow for the production of substances useful to humans. This is the procedure that has been used to produce human insulin.

An organism whose genetic information has been altered by the transfer of genetic material from another species is described as **transgenic**.

Genetically modified plants

There are several ways in which we might choose to genetically modify plants. We might create brighter flowers, introduce different scents, and create more flavoursome food crops or crops resistant to disease. In fact selective breeding, which humans have been practising for centuries, is a form of genetic modification and this has allowed us to produce varieties of plant better adapted to certain situations. The new techniques can simply do the job faster.

The production of new varieties of disease-resistant crops has obvious benefits. It should allow us to grow larger amounts of food more cheaply. If plants are able to resist the diseases caused by certain pests then we will be able to use less pesticide. This should cost less and may also provide a health advantage to farmers who will not be exposed to the same levels of pesticides as before.

There are concerns, however, that genetically modifying crops may lead to problems. The genes that code for resistance could spread from the modified crop species to another closely related wild one. This plant would then have an advantage over other plants and this could unbalance ecosystems.

There are also concerns that in introducing new genes into food crops we may unwittingly introduce something harmful to human health.

QUESTIONS

Q1 What do you think the term 'complementary base pairing' refers to with regard to the structure of DNA?

Q2 In the process of genetic modification what is used to:
  a cut the desired gene out of a strand of DNA?
  b join pieces of DNA together?

More questions on the CD ROM

Q3 What does the term 'transgenic' mean?

Answers are on page 163.

CLONING

Plants

The offspring of a plant will not always have the features of the original. A simple way of producing new **plants** that are genetically identical to the original is by taking **cuttings**. A cutting is a shoot or branch that is removed from the original and planted in soil to grow on its own. Some plants do this easily, others may need rooting hormones to encourage them to grow roots.

A more modern version of taking cuttings is **tissue culture**. This is used to grow large numbers of plants quickly as only a **tiny part** of the original is needed to grow a new plant. This method is also called **micropropagation**. Special procedures have to be followed.

1 Many small pieces are cut from the chosen plant. These pieces are called **explants**.

2 The pieces are **sterilised** by washing them in mild bleach to kill any microbes.

3 In sterile conditions the explants are transferred onto a jelly-like growth medium that contains nutrients as well as plant hormones to encourage growth.

4 The explants should develop roots and shoots and leaves.

5 When the plants are large enough they can be transferred to other growth media and eventually to a normal growth medium like compost.

A small cutting from a geranium has been encouraged to grow fresh roots.

These tiny sundew plants have all grown from tiny cuttings of a single plant.

Animals

Cloning can also now be used with **animals**. For example, cells from a developing **embryo** (such as from a cow) can be split apart before they become specialised and then transplanted, as identical embryos, into **host mothers**.

Another way of cloning animals involves making ordinary **body cells** grow into new animals. Dolly the sheep was the first mammal clone grown from the cell of a fully grown organism: in Dolly's case it was a cell from the udder of a sheep.

There are several potential uses of cloned transgenic animals. These include:

* Research
  Animals created in this way could be better models for human disease. 'Lower species', e.g. mice could be used rather than 'higher species', e.g. non-human primates.

* Drug production
  Transgenic animals could be used in the production of human antibodies or other human proteins for use as medicinal drugs.

* Disease control
  It may be possible to modify pests to prevent them spreading diseases, e.g. to create mosquitoes that no longer carry malaria.

* Food production
  Animals could be engineered to convert their food to meat more efficiently or to produce healthier meat.

* Organ production
  Pigs can be genetically modified to produce organs suitable for human transplantation. This could help to overcome shortages of human donors.

While there are many potential advantages in the use of transgenic animals there are also concerns about the use of animals in this way. There are concerns for the welfare of the animals involved and concerns that such modifications may have unforeseen and unwelcome effects.

QUESTIONS

Q1 What are the advantages and disadvantages of producing new roses by tissue culture (cloning)?

Q2 Dolly the sheep was the first mammal to be the clone of a fully grown adult. Where did the genetic material come from that produced her?

Q3 Suggest one reason why one might want to produce and clone transgenic animals?

More questions on the CD ROM

Answers are on page 163.

Data response answers

Experiment to show the effect of temperature on enzyme activity (page 19)
1 Tube 3.
2 You should draw a line graph with temperature along the x-axis and activity along the y-axis. The points should be joined by a smooth line to give a u-shaped graph.
3 30°C.
4 The temperature damages the structure of the enzyme.
5 Repeat using a range of temperatures between 30 and 40°C.

Experiment to investigate the effect of surface area to volume ratio (page 23)
1 The 0.5cm cube.
2 Penetration of dye would be slower.
3 The dye can only enter at the surface and the surface area is much lower compared with volume for larger bodies.
4 This speeds up absorption of food materials from the gut.

Experiment to make a model gut (page 25)
1 To ensure the solution was not contaminated by sugar.
2 Starch cannot pass through the tubing but sugar can.
3 Yes, sugar is detectable in the water outside the Visking tubing in 10 minutes.

Experiment to investigate changes in weight due to osmosis (page 26)
1 Tube 5
2 You should draw a barchart to display these results with tubes along the x-axis and % weight gain up the y-axis.
3 Water is drawn in by osmosis – increasing its mass.

Experiment to investigate changes in shape due to osmosis (page 27)
1 Those in the dish containing water.
2 No, some strips curl with the outer surface outermost and some curl with it innermost.
3 Water is drawn in by osmosis so making the cells swell. Water is only drawn in on the inner surface of the stalk because the outer surface is covered with a waterproof layer. The cells expand and bend the stalk with the outer surface on the inside of the curve.

Experiment to investigate the requirements for light and carbon dioxide (page 33)
1 Since we are using the presence of starch as a sign of photosynthetic activity we need to make sure all existing starch has been cleared.
2 Light, carbon dioxide, water and chlorophyll.
3 Both chemicals are highly corrosive and can dissolve human skin.

Experiment to investigate light levels and photosynthesis (page 34)
1 The distance of 5cm.
2 The graph should be drawn with distance along the x-axis and light intensity along the y-axis.

Experiment to examine the energy content of a food sample (page 41)
1 The leaf.
2 Because you used different amounts of material so to make the test fair you had to compare equal masses of material.
3 The nut is an energy-storage tissue and will contain more energy than the leaf which does not store large amounts of energy. The leaf sends the fixed sugar to other areas of the plant for storage. Nuts often contain large amounts of oil which is very energy-rich.

Experiment to show the production of carbon dioxide and heat by living organisms (page 44)
1 Carbon dioxide
2 In the control experiment without seeds no change was detected.
3 The amount of heat produced by the germinating seeds is very small. If they were contained in a non-insulated container it would all conduct away before any temperature change could be detected.

Experiment to investigate light levels and net gas exchange in leaf discs (page 46)
1 pH.
2 As the leaf disks carried out photosynthesis they removed carbon dioxide from the solution. This made the pH rise and so the colour change.
3 Respiration occurs in the dark and the light. In the dark the carbon dioxide produced is not immediately used in photosynthesis so it dissolves in the water and makes it more acid. This changes the colour of the indicator.

Experiment to investigate exercise, breathing and pulse rates (page 51)
1 To remove the effect of any events immediately prior to taking the measurements, e.g. the subject may have just run up the stairs to get to the laboratory.
2 (95–65)/65 = 46%
3 Volume processed = breaths per minute x volume per breath
At rest = 3 x 1.9 = 5.7l/min
After exercise = 6 x 3.2 = 19.2l/min

Experiment to investigate transpiration and environmental conditions (page 54)
1 Hot moving air in sunlight
2 257/54 = 4.8 times faster
3 The rate of transpiration is much higher in these conditions.
4 It would slow down or even stop and go backwards.

Experiment to investigate yeasts and anaerobic respiration (page 116)
1 It tends to slow it down and can stop it at high enough concentrations.
2 Repeat the experiment at a range of temperatures.

EXAM PRACTICE AND ANSWERS

EXAM TIPS

Read each question carefully; this includes looking in detail at any diagrams, graphs or tables.
* Remember that any information you are given is there to help you.
* Underline or circle the key words in the question and make sure you answer the question that is being asked.

Make sure that you understand the meaning of the 'command words' in the questions. For example:
* 'Describe' is used when you have to give the main feature(s) of, for example, a process or structure;
* 'Explain' is used when you have to give reasons, e.g. for some experimental results;
* 'Suggest' is used when there may be more than one possible answer, or when you will not have learnt the answer but have to use the knowledge you do have to come up with a sensible one;
* 'Calculate' means that you have to work out an answer in figures.

Look at the number of marks allocated to each question and also the space provided.
* Include at least as many points in your answer as there are marks. If you do need more space to answer, then use the nearest available space, e.g. at the bottom of the page, making sure you write down which question you are answering. Beware of continually writing too much because it probably means you are not really answering the questions.

Don't spend so long on some questions that you don't have time to finish the paper.
* You should spend approximately one minute per mark. If you are really stuck on a question, leave it, finish the rest of the paper and come back to it at the end.

In short answer questions, or multiple-choice type questions, don't write more than you are asked for.
* In some exams, examiners apply the rule that they only mark the first part of the answer written if there is too much. This means that the later part of the answer will not be looked at.
* In other exams you would not gain any marks if you have written something incorrect in the later part of your answer, even if the first part of your answer is correct. This just shows that you have not really understood the question or are guessing.

In calculations always show your working.
* Even if your final answer is incorrect you may still gain some marks if part of your attempt is correct. If you just write down the final answer and it is incorrect, you will get no marks at all.
* Also in calculations write your answer to as many significant figures as are used in the question.
* You may also lose marks if you do not use the correct units.

Aim to use good English and scientific language to make your answer as clear as possible.

- In short answer questions, just one or two words may be enough, but in longer answers take particular care with capital letters, commas and full stops.
- There should be an icon in the margin to warn you where there are separate marks for the quality of your English.
- If it helps you to answer clearly, do not be afraid to also use diagrams in your answers.

Some questions will be about scientific ideas and how scientists use evidence.

- In these questions you may be given some information about an unfamiliar situation.
- The answers to this type of question usually link to one of four areas: how scientists communicate their ideas; how scientific ideas can reflect the society in which the scientists work; how scientists can give different interpretations to the same evidence; how science can answer some questions but not others.

When you have finished your exam, check through to make sure you have answered all the questions.

- Cover your answers and read through the questions again and check your answers are as good as you can make them.

EXAM QUESTIONS AND STUDENTS' ANSWERS (FOUNDATION TIER)

1 When athletes run races they get energy from aerobic respiration and from anaerobic respiration. The table below shows the percentage of energy from aerobic and anaerobic respiration in races of different length.

Length of race	Percentage of energy	
	Aerobic respiration	**Anaerobic respiration**
100 m	5	95
1 500 m	55	45
10 000 m	90	10
Marathon (42 186 m)	98	2

a) i) What percentage of energy is provided by anaerobic respiration in a 10 000 m race?

Answer _10_ % [1]

ii) In how many of the races does aerobic respiration provide a greater percentage of energy? [1]

three [1]

carbon dioxide	energy	glucose
lactic acid	oxygen	water

b) Use words from the box to complete the sentences below.

Aerobic respiration uses _oxygen_ and _glucose_ to produce a lot of energy.
The two waste products are _carbon dioxide_ and _water_ . [4]

[Total 7 marks]

2 The table shows the effect of increasing temperature on the yield of a crop.

Temperature in °C	Crop yield in kg per 100 m^2
10	5
20	11
30	24
40	10
50	7

a) i) Plot the data in the table on the following grid and join the points with straight lines. [4]

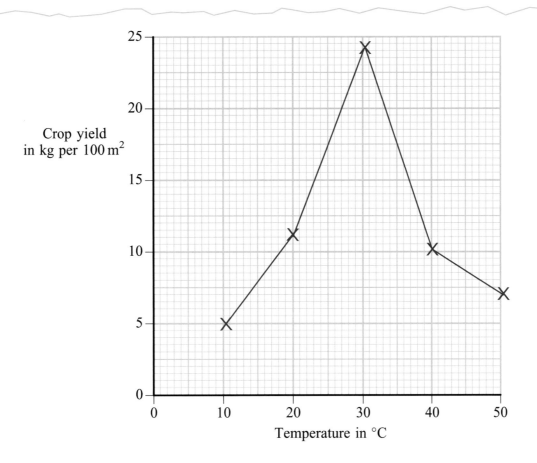

ii) Use your graph to find the crop yield at 25 °C.

_17.5_____ kg per 100 m² [1]

iii) Describe what happens to the yield of this crop as the temperature increases.

Yield increases with increasing temperature between 0 and 30 °C
but decreases with increasing temperature beyond 30 °C. [2]

b) Suggest **two** other ways that a farmer could increase the yield of a crop.

1 He could water the crops regularly to provide water for photosynthesis
and growth.
2 He could spray the crops with herbicides, which kill weeds that compete
with the crop for nutrients. [2]

[Total 9 marks]

3 a) The table lists types of cell found in the human body.
Complete the table by writing the number of chromosomes found in each cell.
The first one has been done for you.

Name of cell	Number of chromosomes in cell
neurone	46
sperm	23
red blood cell	0
skin	46

[3]

b) Sperm cells are needed for fertilisation.
   i) In what part of the body are sperm cells made?
   the testes [1]

   ii) Name the other type of cell involved in fertilisation.
   ovum (egg) [1]

[Total 5 marks]

HOW TO SCORE FULL MARKS

Make sure you read the questions carefully and don't confuse words that look similar such as aerobic and anaerobic.

Look at the number of marks available for each part of the question. There is no point in spending a lot of time writing a detailed answer for only one mark. A single word may be all that is required.

On the other hand, if part of a section is for 2 marks you should try to give two facts.
E.g.
iii) Describe what happens to the yield of this crop as the temperature increases.

Yield increases with increasing temperature between 0 and 30 °C but decreases with increasing temperature beyond 30 °C.

Here you need to describe both the initial increase in yield and the subsequent decrease. If a question asks you to give a specific number of details don't give more than is asked for. Question 2 b asks for two other ways in which a farmer could increase the yield of his crop. You may know several things he could do but if you list all those things you will only be marked for the first two given. Choose the two that you consider most important or that you feel most confident about.

QUESTIONS TO TRY (FOUNDATION TIER)

1 Genetically modified (GM) bacteria can be grown in a large container called a fermenter. The graph shows the numbers of live GM bacteria in a fermenter over 32 hours.

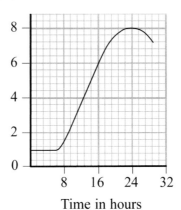

Number of living bacteria in hundreds of millions

Time in hours

a)   i)   How many hours did it take to produce **600 million** bacteria?

   _____ [1]

   ii)   What was the highest number of living bacteria in the fermenter?

   _____ [1]

   iii)   How many GM bacteria were in the fermenter at the start?

   _____ [2]

   iv)   Put an **X** on the graph to show when the bacteria are reproducing fastest.

   _____ [1]

   v)   Suggest **two** reasons why the number of living GM bacteria fell after 24 hours.

   1 _____

   2 _____ [2]

b)   GM bacteria can be used to make a human hormone.
   Which of the hormones in the box helps lower blood glucose levels and can be made by GM bacteria?

| adrenaline | insulin | testosterone | oestrogen |
[1]

[Total 8 marks]

2 The diagram shows a food web.

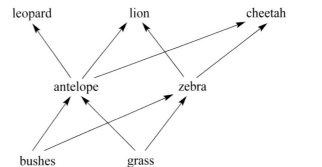

a)   Name **one** producer in the food web.

   _____   [1]

b)   Name **one** secondary consumer in the food web.

   _____   [1]

c) Using the information in the food web, draw **one** food chain with **three** organisms in it.

_____ [2]

d) There is a disease that has killed all zebras.
What will happen to the number of lions? Give a reason for your answer.

_____

_____

_____ [2]

[Total 6 marks]

3 A person sat down to rest for one hour. Twenty minutes after sitting down the person smoked a cigarette. The table shows the pulse rate of the person every 10 minutes during this hour.

Time in minutes	Pulse rate in beats per minute
0	65
10	65
20	65
30	95
40	85
50	75
60	65

a) i) Plot the data in the table on the grid below. Join the points with straight lines.

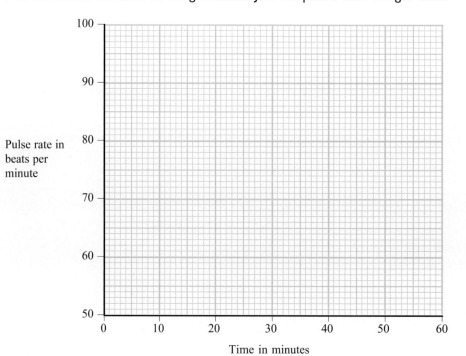

Pulse rate in beats per minute

Time in minutes

[2]

  ii) How does smoking a cigarette affect pulse rate?

  _____ [1]

  iii) How many minutes did it take for the pulse rate to return to normal after
       smoking the cigarette if it takes 10 minutes to smoke the cigarette?

  _____ [1]

b) The table below gives three types of blood vessel in the human body.
    Which type of blood vessel is used to measure pulse rate?
    Tick (✓) the correct answer.

Blood vessel	Tick
artery	
capillary	
vein	

[1]

c) Smoking cigarettes can harm the body. In which organ may bronchitis and
    cancer occur?

[1]

[Total 6 marks]

More questions
on the CD ROM

Answers are on page 155.

EXAM QUESTIONS AND STUDENTS' ANSWERS (FOUNDATION/HIGHER TIER OVERLAP)

1 The diagram below shows the female reproductive system.

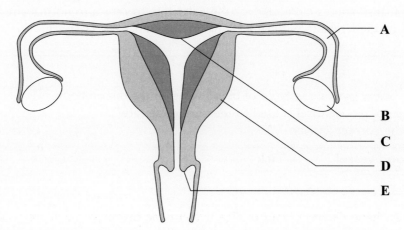

The table below lists some events that occur in the female reproductive system. Complete the table using letters from the diagram to show the part where each event occurs.

Write **one** letter only in each box. A letter may be used once, more than once, or not at all.

Event	Letter
Eggs produced	B
Fertilisation occurs	A
Placenta forms	C
Progesterone secreted	B

2 Certain cells lining the pancreatic duct produce mucus. In people who inherit cystic fibrosis these cells produce very sticky mucus. This sticky mucus blocks the pancreatic duct.

The gene for mucus production has two alleles. The allele for producing normal mucus, **N**, is dominant to the allele for producing very sticky mucus, **n**.

a) Two parents are heterozygous for this gene. They had four children.
  i) In the box below give the genotype of one of the parents.

  Nn

  [1]

  ii) The boxes below show the genotypes of their four children. Put a circle around the box showing the genotype of a child with cystic fibrosis.

   NN   Nn Nn   nn

  [1]

  iii) How many of the children are homozygous?

  2 _____

  [1]

b) People with cystic fibrosis cannot easily digest their food because the digestive enzymes they need are not present in part of the small intestine (duodenum). One way of treating cystic fibrosis is for people to take tablets containing digestive enzymes with their meals. The diagram shows a section through a tablet.

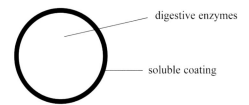
digestive enzymes

soluble coating

i) Suggest why the digestive enzymes are not present in the duodenum.

They cannot be released from the pancreas because the duct is blocked by sticky mucus   [1]

ii) Suggest **three** different types of digestive enzyme that might be in the tablet.

1 *proteases*

2 *lipases*

3 *amylases*   [3]

iii) It is important that the soluble coating does not dissolve until the tablet has passed through the stomach. Suggest why the enzymes in the tablet might not work if they had been released in the stomach.

the enzymes are proteins and so would be denatured by the stomach acid and protease enzymes in the stomach   [2]

[Total 9 marks]

3 A river is poisoned by some raw sewage. This causes changes in the number of micro-organisms in the river. This in turn has an effect on the number of large fish in the river.
Describe and explain these changes.

Raw sewage acts like excess fertiliser in the river stimulating the growth of algae. The algae use up oxygen in the river and block out sunlight so that the normal aquatic plants begin to die. The dead plants provide food for micro-organisms which use up more of the oxygen. There is not enough oxygen in the water for the large fish and they begin to die.

[total 5 marks]

HOW TO SCORE FULL MARKS

Remember to read the question carefully. Question 1 asks you to write one letter only in each box. If you put more than one letter in the box you will get no marks even if one letter is correct. Note that a letter may be used once, more than once, or not at all – don't automatically think you must use all the letters and only once each.

If you get stuck for an answer, try rereading the question. For example Question 2 here gives you a

lot of information. Even if you hadn't remembered the answer to part b (i) you could guess it from the details given in the question.

Question 3 doesn't have separate parts. Sometimes it is difficult to decide how much detail is required for an answer like this. Look at the mark allocation. Try to think of a different fact for each mark then put them together to give a clear, simple story. You do not need to write a long essay.

QUESTIONS TO TRY (FOUNDATION/HIGHER TIER OVERLAP)

1 The diagram shows part of the human digestive system.

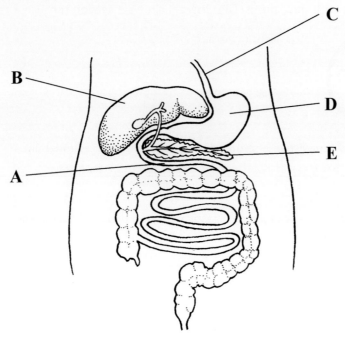

a) The table below lists some processes that occur in the human digestive system. Complete the table using letters from the diagram to show where each process occurs.

Write **one** letter only in each box.

Process	Letter
protein is first digested	
fat is emulsified	
bile is produced	
insulin is released	

[4]

b) i) Name the process by which muscles move food through the gut.

_____ [1]

ii) What biological term describes the process of removing undigested food from the body?

_____ [1]

[Total 6 marks]

2 a) Cells can divide by mitosis. The diagram below shows the chromosomes in a parent cell before mitosis takes place.

     i) Complete the diagram to show the chromosomes in each daughter cell.

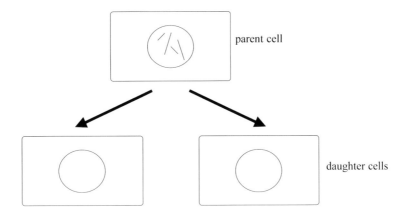

          [1]

     ii) What is the diploid number of the parent cell?

_____ [1]

b) The graph below shows the time taken for cells to divide by mitosis at different temperatures.

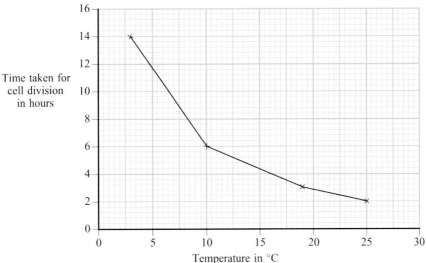

     i) How does the increase in temperature affect the time taken for cell division to occur?

_____ [1]

     ii) Starting with one cell, at 25 °C, how many cells would there be after

       2 hours _____

       8 hours _____ [2]

[Total 5 marks]

3 Farmers have attempted to increase the yield of crop plants by the use of glasshouses and fertiliser.

Explain how the use of glasshouses and fertiliser can result in an increase in crop yield.

_____

_____

_____

_____

_____

_____

_____

_____

_____

[Total 6 marks]

More questions
on the CD ROM

Answers are on pages 155–6.

EXAM QUESTIONS AND STUDENTS' ANSWERS (HIGHER TIER)

1 The flow chart shows some of the stages in making beer.

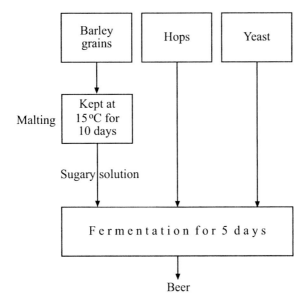

a) A sugary solution is made from the barley grains during the malting process. Describe how sugar is made in the barley grains.

Starch is stored inside the barley grains. The starch is broken down into sugar by enzymes. [2]

b) Yeast is added to the sugary solution to ferment it. Describe what happens to the sugar during fermentation.

The sugar is converted into alcohol. [2]

c) Brewers use different varieties of hops in their products. Suggest why.

Different hops will produce different flavours for beer. [1]

[Total 5 marks]

HOW TO SCORE FULL MARKS

a) Both marks have been awarded. The student has clearly described how barley grains made sugar.

b) Always look at the number of marks available for an answer. The student gained one of the two marks available. The student could have gained the other mark for stating that fermentation is a type of anaerobic respiration. A mark could also have been awarded for stating that part of the sugar produces carbon dioxide.

c) This question says 'suggest', so the student has to apply knowledge to the topic. The student gains a mark for the answer of different flavours. A mark could also have been given for a comment about different hops causing different bitterness of taste.

2 The drawing shows a cactus plant.

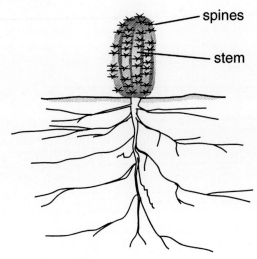

This cactus plant lives in a hot, dry desert.

The leaves have evolved to become spines.

The stem is green.

a) i) Plants have roots to take in water. This cactus plant has very long roots. Suggest how very long roots help cactus plants to survive in dry desert conditions.

Long roots can absorb more water [1]

   ii) Describe two other jobs of roots.

     1 _to hold the plant in the ground_

     2 _to take in minerals from the soil_ [2]

   iii) Write down the name of the transport tissue that carries water from the roots to the rest of the plant.

xylem [1]

b) Is a cactus plant a producer or a consumer? Explain your answer.

The cactus plant is a producer because it can photosynthesise to produce its
own food [1]

c) The spines (leaves) of a cactus plant are not very efficient at photosynthesis. Explain why.

They have a small surface area

[2]

[Total 7 marks]

HOW TO SCORE FULL MARKS

a) i) A mark would be given for any one from: long roots can absorb more water or absorb water faster; large roots can collect water from a large area; they can compete for water and can help the plant to survive when water is scarce; large roots can store water. A common error is to say that roots take in food. Do not forget the important fact that green plants have to make their own food.

   ii) A mark each would be given for any two from: anchorage; water storage; take in minerals. The question asks for two **other** jobs: check that you do not write a fact that has already been given.

   iii) It is easy to confuse xylem and phloem. Try to remember that x and w are close together in the alphabet, and xylem carries water; phloem carries the food (glucose) for the plant.

b) This answer is worth one mark. The mark is for the explanation, not for the answer 'producer'. Marks are not awarded for a choice from two, such as producer or consumer.

c) A mark each would be given for any two from: they have a small surface area; less light can be absorbed; they have less chlorophyll; they have very few stomata; very little carbon dioxide is taken in. The student only gained one of the two marks available. The student only wrote one comment. The question did not ask for two comments, but two marks were allocated to it. Always check the marks awarded, in brackets at the end of the lines. Two marks will require two pieces of information.

---

3 A plant leaf was exposed to radioactive carbon dioxide as shown in the diagram below.

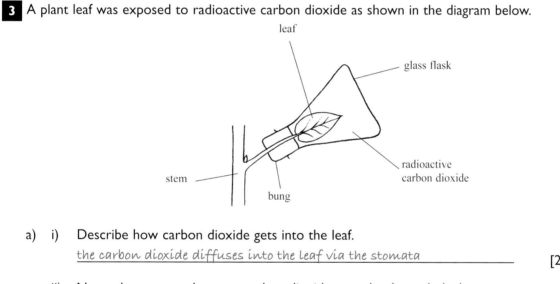

a) i) Describe how carbon dioxide gets into the leaf.

   the carbon dioxide diffuses into the leaf via the stomata   [2]

   ii) Name the process that uses carbon dioxide to make the carbohydrate.

   photosynthesis.   [1]

b) The amount of carbohydrate transported to other parts of the plant can be found by measuring the amount of radioactivity.

   i) Name the tissue that transports the carbohydrate.

   phloem   [1]

   ii) Name the carbohydrate that is transported in this tissue.

   sucrose   [1]

c) The table below shows the amount of radioactivity in different parts of the plant after 24 hours.

Part of plant	Amount of radioactivity in counts per minute
shoot tip	1123
leaf exposed to radioactive carbon dioxide	11 325
other leaves	234
stem	819
seeds	9 055
roots	842

i) What evidence in the table shows that carbohydrate is transported both up and down the plant?

radioactivity is detected in the roots and the shoot tips [1]

ii) Suggest why the "other leaves" contain only small amounts of radioactive carbohydrate.

This is carbohydrate that was made in the experimental leaf and transported here via the phloem. Most of the carbohydrate present in the leaves will have been produced in the leaves using non-radioactive carbon dioxide. [1]

iii) Ignoring the leaf that was exposed, calculate how much more radioactive carbohydrate was found in the seeds than in all the other plant parts added together.

_6037_ counts per minute [1]

iv) Explain why a supply of carbohydrate is needed for the uptake of minerals by roots.

Uptake of minerals is against a concentration gradient. This involves active transport, which requires energy. The energy is generated by cellular respiration, which requires glucose and oxygen. The glucose comes from the sucrose and starch generated by the plant during photosynthesis.

[3]

[Total 11 marks]

4 Farmers can improve their crop plants or farm animals by the use of selective breeding.
Explain what is meant by 'selective breeding' and give **two** examples of its use.

In selective breeding a farmer selects plants or animals to breed from because they have good characteristics. Over time this increases the prevalence of the characteristic in the population of his herd or food crop.

Dairy cows can be selected for breeding on the basis of their milk yield. In this case only high-yielding cows are allowed to have calves.

A food plant could be selected for breeding because it showed resistance to a certain disease.

[Total 6 marks]

HOW TO SCORE FULL MARKS

Remember to read the questions carefully and look at the mark allocation. For example Question 3 a (i) is for two marks so you need to give a little more detail than just 'by diffusion'. If you feel you really don't know the answer to part of a question don't waste too much time over it. Answer the questions you feel confident about and then come back to the one you were stuck on.

QUESTIONS TO TRY (HIGHER TIER)

I Cystic fibrosis is an inherited disease in which certain cells produce abnormal mucus.
The allele for the disease is recessive.
The diagram shows how cystic fibrosis was inherited in one family.

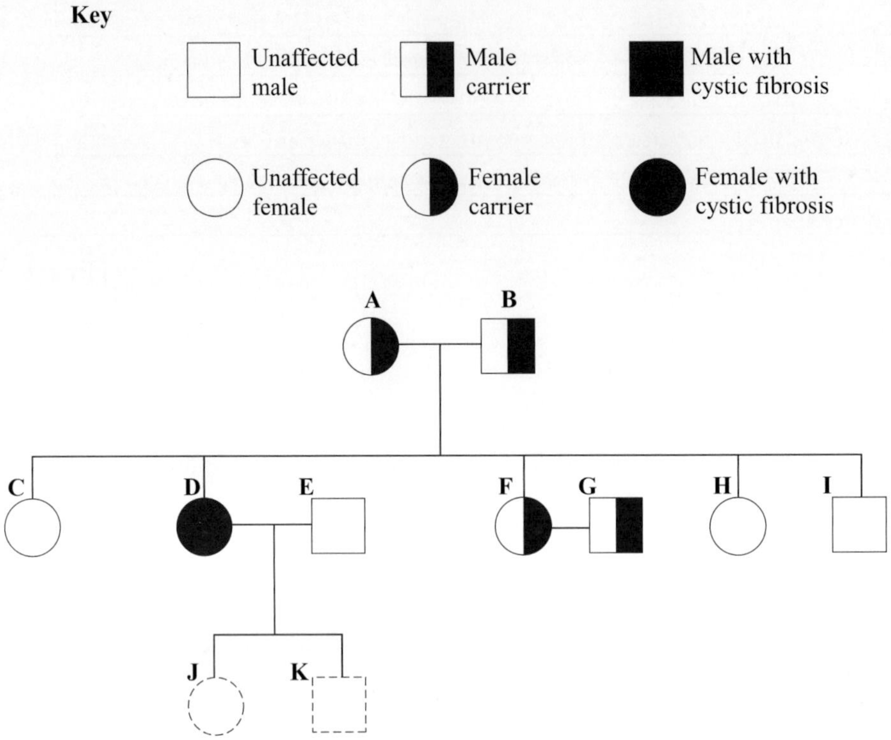

Key

☐ Unaffected male   ◨ Male carrier   ■ Male with cystic fibrosis

○ Unaffected female   ◖ Female carrier   ● Female with cystic fibrosis

a) Complete the diagram by correctly shading the symbols for person **J** and
person **K**.   [1]

b) Persons **A** and **B** are carriers.
What does this mean? _____
_____
_____   [2]

c) How many of the children of **A** and **B** were homozygous dominant?
_____   [1]

d) What is the phenotype of **D**?
_____   [1]

e) What is the probability of **F** and **G** having a child with cystic fibrosis?
_____   [1]

f) What is the probability of **F** and **G** having a male child with cystic fibrosis?
_____   [1]

[Total 7 marks]

2 a) What word is used to describe water loss from the leaves of a plant?

_____ [1]

b) Loss of water from a leafy shoot can be measured using the apparatus below.

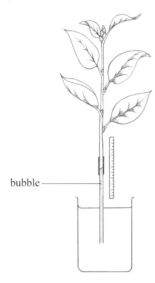

bubble

This apparatus was used by a student, in a brightly lit room, to measure the rate of water loss from a leafy shoot. He measured how far the bubble moved in five minutes. He measured this three times.
The results are shown in the table.

Measurement	Distance moved by the bubble in cm
1	11.9
2	12.6
3	13.0

i) Use these results to calculate the mean (average) rate of water loss in cm per minute. Show your working.

Answer _____ cm per minute. [2]

ii) If the room became colder, explain what would happen to the distance moved by the bubble.

_____
_____
_____
_____ [2]

iii) If the light intensity became lower, explain what would happen to the distance moved by the bubble.

_____

_____

_____

_____ [2]

c) Another student investigated the rate of water loss using a similar sized leafy shoot from a different species of plant. She noticed that the upper and lower surfaces of these leaves were covered with tiny hairs.
Suggest how these hairs would affect the rate of water loss from this leafy shoot.

_____

_____

_____

_____ [2]

[Total 9 marks]

3 Gas exchange takes place in the lungs.
The diagram shows an alveolus and a capillary. The numbers on the diagram represent the concentration of oxygen (in arbitrary units) in the alveolus and at different places in the capillary. The arrows show the direction of blood flow in the capillary.

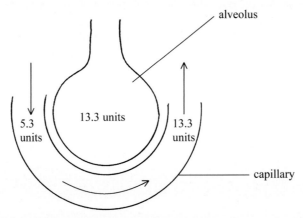

a) Explain why the concentration of oxygen in the blood changes as it travels along the capillary.

_____

_____

_____ [2]

b) The formula shows how to calculate a value that represents oxygen uptake between the lung and the blood.

$$\text{oxygen uptake} = \frac{\text{SA} \times \text{oxygen difference}}{\text{distance}}$$

SA = total surface area of alveoli in m^2

oxygen difference = difference in oxygen concentration between the alveoli and the blood entering the capillary in arbitrary units

distance = distance gas molecules travel from the alveoli into the blood in mm

i) The total surface area in a normal human lung is 120 m². The distance between an alveolus and the blood is 0.1 mm.
Use this information, the information in the diagram, and the formula, to calculate the value for oxygen uptake in a normal lung.
Show your working.

[2]

ii) Emphysema is a lung disease caused by smoking cigarettes. The diagrams below show the alveoli in a normal lung and the alveoli in the lung of a person with emphysema.

alveoli in normal lung   alveoli in the lung of a person with emphysema

What effect would emphysema have on the value for oxygen uptake?

_____ [1]

iii) Suggest how the air this person breathes can be altered to relieve the symptoms of emphysema.

_____ [1]

[Total 6 marks]

4 DNA is a double helix with each strand linked by a series of paired bases. There are four bases in DNA.
The table below shows the percentage of each base found in a sample of DNA taken from a mammal. Only two of the bases have been named in the table.

a) Complete the table to give the names of the other two bases.

Percentage of base in DNA sample	Name of base
30	thymine (T)
20	guanine (G)
30	
20	

[2]

b) The sample of DNA contained 2000 bases. How many thymine bases would the DNA sample contain?

_____ [1]

c) Human DNA contains the gene to make insulin. Bacteria can be modified to contain this gene. Describe the steps used to do this.

_____
_____
_____
_____
_____
_____
_____
_____
_____
_____ [5]

[Total 8 marks]

More questions
on the CD ROM

Answers are on page 156.

EXAM QUESTIONS AND STUDENTS' ANSWERS (COMMON IN BOTH TIER)

1 The following steps describe the procedure used to show that a green leaf contains starch.

- The steps are **not** in the correct order.
- Add iodine solution
- Immerse in boiling water for 1 minute
- Heat leaf in boiling ethanol
- Place plant in bright sunshine for 12 hours
- Place plant in darkness for 24 hours
- Remove leaf from plant

a) Fill in the table below to show these steps in the correct order. Then, in the table, give a reason why each step is carried out. Some parts of the table have been filled in for you.

Step	Reason why carried out
1. Place plant in darkness for 24 hours	*Ensures all starch in the plant is removed.*
2. *Place plant in bright sunshine for 12 hours*	Allows photosynthesis to occur
3. Remove leaf from plant	*Allows starch test to be performed*
4. *Immerse in boiling water for 1 minute*	Kills leaf, bursts cells
5. *Heat leaf in boiling ethanol*	*Removes chlorophyll*
6. *Add iodine solution*	Shows the presence of starch

[7]

b) In one of the steps the leaf is boiled in ethanol. Describe how you could carry this out safely.

Ethanol should not be heated directly because it is highly flammable.
Place a tube of ethanol in a beaker of hot water (about 70 °C).

[1]

[Total 8 marks]

2 Anna carried out an investigation into photosynthesis in which she varied the concentration of carbon dioxide available to a water plant. She added different masses of sodium hydrogencarbonate to the water. She was careful to control all other key factors that might affect the rate of photosynthesis. The apparatus she used is shown in the diagram below.

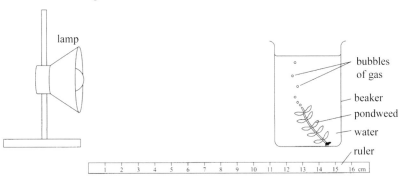

She predicted that increasing the carbon dioxide concentration would increase the rate of photosynthesis.

She observed the water plant and counted the bubbles coming off. She did this for 3 minutes for each concentration of sodium hydrogencarbonate.

Table 1

Number of bubbles of oxygen released each minute	Mass of sodium hydrogencarbonate added to the beaker in g				
	0	1	1.5	2	2.5
Minute 1	4	16	29	43	60
Minute 2	3	17	31	29	63
Minute 3	4	15	25	28	57

a) She decided to calculate the average number of bubbles released for each mass of sodium hydrogencarbonate added.
She recorded her results for this calculation and these are given in table 2.

Table 2

Mass of sodium hydrogencarbonate in g	Average number of bubbles released per minute
0	3.67
1.0	16.00
1.5	28.33
2.0	33.3
2.5	60.00

Calculate the average value for the 2.0 g data. Insert your value in the space in table 2. [1]

b) i) Anna's experiment looked at the effect of different concentrations of carbon dioxide. Name one other key factor that could influence the rate of photosynthesis.

    <u>Light intensity</u> [1]

    ii) For this factor state how Anna could ensure that it does not affect the rate of photosynthesis in her experiment.

    <u>Make sure the beaker is kept at a constant distance from the lamp</u> [1]

c) i) Using information in table 2, write a suitable conclusion for Anna's experiment. You should include the effect of increasing hydrogencarbonate concentration on the number of bubbles released.

    <u>As the amount of carbon dioxide increases (with increasing</u>
    <u>concentration of hydrogencarbonate), the rate of photosynthesis</u>
    <u>increases, shown by the higher number of bubbles released.</u> [1]

    ii) Give an explanation of these results using your scientific knowledge.
    <u>Carbon dioxide is needed for photosynthesis.</u> [1]

    iii) Relate the results to Anna's prediction.

Anna's prediction was correct.   [1]

d)   Comment on any unexpected results or pattern of results in table 1.

With 2 g hydrogencarbonate, there were more bubbles of oxygen released in the first minute than in the second and third minute.   [1]

e) i) Suggest **one** way that this experiment could be modified to improve the reliability or accuracy of the results. Explain how your modification could improve the results.

Modification

Collect the gas in a measuring cylinder or graduated tube

Explanation

This allows the amount of oxygen produced to measured accurately and quantitatively   [2]

   ii) Suggest a further experiment that you could carry out and explain how it would provide more information on the effect of carbon dioxide on photosynthesis.

Continue to increase the amount of hydrogencarbonate added to the water to see if carbon dioxide availability becomes a limiting factor for photosynthesis   [2]

[Total 11 marks]

3 Describe an investigation you could carry out to find out what effect exercise has on breathing rate.
You should include full experimental details in your account.

1. *A number of people of the same sex, age and build should be selected as experimental subjects. They should be as similar as possible to avoid too many variables. The conditions in which the investigation is to be performed should remain constant e.g. no temperature fluctuations.*
2. *The normal breathing rate of the experimental subjects at rest should be measured and recorded. This can be done by counting the number of breaths taken in a five minute period and dividing by five to get a value for average number of breaths per minute.*
3. *The subjects should then perform some exercise such as stepping up onto a bench and down again over a period of two minutes.*
4. *The breathing rate should be measured again as described in step 1.*
5. *The results should be recorded. The experiment could be repeated after allowing the subjects breathing rate to return to normal.*
6. *The investigation could be repeated with different levels of exercise.*

[Total 4 marks]

QUESTIONS TO TRY (PAPER 3)

1 Asha wanted to test some foods.
Her teacher told her the following reagents were available.

| Biuret | Benedict's | ethanol | iodine solution |

a) Choose the reagent Asha should use to test foods for starch.

_____ [1]

b) Asha used the table below to show her results.
Complete the table by writing the colour she obtained for each food.

Food	Colour obtained	Starch present
bread		yes
milk		no

[2]

c) Asha decided to test her foods for glucose.
   i) Describe the test she would do.

   _____

   _____

   _____ [2]

   i) What result would she see if glucose was present?

   _____ [1]

   iii) Suggest how she might use the results to say how much glucose was present.

   _____

   _____ [1]

   [Total 7 marks]

2 David carried out an investigation into the effect of temperature on anaerobic respiration in yeast. The only factor that he changed was the temperature of the reaction mixture. He was careful to control all other key factors that might affect the rate of respiration in yeast. David predicted that the rate of respiration in yeast would increase as the temperature increased. The apparatus he used is shown in the diagram.

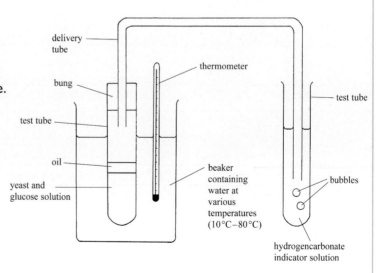

David counted the bubbles of carbon dioxide being given off in one minute as the yeast respired.

He did this three times for each temperature he used.

a) Why did David put oil on the surface of the yeast and glucose solution?

_____ [1]

b) State **one** key factor that David should control and suggest how he might do this.

Factor   _____

How controlled   _____

_____ [2]

c) David put his results into a table.

Temperature in °C	Number of bubbles of carbon dioxide released in one minute			
	First count	Second count	Third count	Average
10	10	10	9	9.7
20	21	22	20	21.0
30	40	38	41	39.7
40	55	54	53	
50	60	65	64	63.0
60	54	52	30	45.3
70	31	30	29	30.0
80	0	0	0	0.0

i) Calculate the average number of bubbles released in one minute at 40 °C. Write your answer in the empty box in the results table.

[1]

ii) Using the results in the table, describe the effect of increasing the temperature on the rate of respiration in yeast.

_____

_____

_____

_____ [2]

iii) David had predicted that the rate of respiration in yeast would increase as the temperature increased. To what extent do his results support this prediction?

_____

_____

_____

_____ [2]

iv) Using your biological knowledge, explain the average result at 80 °C.

_____

_____

_____

_____ [2]

d) Identify **one** anomalous (unexpected) result in David's table.

_____ [1]

_____

e) i) Suggest **one** way that this experiment could be modified to improve the reliability or accuracy of the results. Explain how your modification could improve the results.
Modification

_____

_____

Explanation

_____

_____ [2]

ii) Suggest a further experiment David could carry out and explain how it would provide more information on the effect of temperature on respiration in yeast.

_____

_____

_____

_____ [2]

[Total 15 marks]

3 Describe how you could compare the population size of a plant growing in two different places. One place is on the side of a hill and the other place is on a piece of flat ground.

_____

_____

_____

_____

_____

_____

_____

_____

_____

_____

_____

_____ [4]

More questions on the CD ROM

Answers are on page 157.

EXAM PRACTICE

Foundation Tier (pages 131–3)

Q1 a) i) 16 hours

ii) 800 million

iii) 100 million

iv)

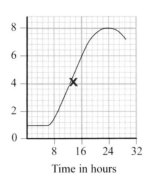

Number of living bacteria in hundreds of millions

Time in hours

v) 1 There may not be enough nutrients left to support such a high population.

2 Waste products, which may be toxic, will have built up.

b) insulin

Q2 a) Grass OR bushes

The question asks for **one** producer, so you could have written either bushes or grass, but not both.

b) Leopard OR lion OR cheetah

The question asks for **one** secondary consumer, so you could have written any one of the three animals in the top row (leopard, lion or cheetah) but not all three.

c) Grass → Zebra → Cheetah

There are many possible answers to this question. The food chain should have one producer (grass or bushes), one primary consumer (antelope or zebra) and one secondary consumer (leopard, lion, cheetah), following the arrows (note from the diagram that leopards do not eat zebra).

d) Lions eat antelope as well as zebra so they still have a food source. They would have to compete with the other carnivores for the antelope, so the number of lions may decrease as there is less food available. (The antelope will not have to compete with the zebra for food so their population could increase; however this would take time and in the meantime both the cheetah and lion populations will be preying on them.)

Q3 a) i)

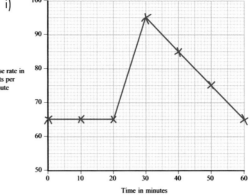

Pulse rate in beats per minute

Time in minutes

ii) Smoking a cigarette increases the heart rate.

iii) 30 minutes

b) Tick ✓ the correct answer.

Blood vessel	Tick ✓
artery	✓
capillary	
vein	

c) the lungs

Foundation/Higher Tier Overlap (pages 136–8)

Q1 a)

Process	Letter
protein is first digested	D
fat is emulsified	A
bile is produced	B
insulin is release	E

b) i) peristalsis

ii) egestion

Q2 i)

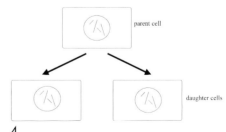

parent cell

daughter cells

ii) 4

b) i) As the temperature increases the time taken for cell division decreases, i.e. cell division gets quicker.

ii) after 2 hours there would be 2 cells [1 cell division]

after 8 hours there would be 16 cells [4 cell divisions]

155

Q3 Glasshouse protect plants from variations in the environment and provide a higher temperature for growth. Because the rate of metabolic reactions increases with temperature (until the temperature becomes too high), increasing temperature increases growth. Plants need certain nutrients for healthy growth including nitrogen, potassium and phosphorus. Nitrogen is particularly important because it is used in the production of proteins and chlorophyll. Fertilisers can help to supply the correct balance of nutrients for maximum production.

Higher Tier (pages 144–8)

Q1 a) J

K

b) They have only one copy of the cystic fibrosis gene (they are heterozygous). This means that they do not have cystic fibrosis, but they can pass the gene on to their children.

c) 3 [C, H and I – homozygous dominant means they do not have CF]

d) Female with cystic fibrosis

e) 1 in 4 or 25%

f) 1 in 8 or 12.5%

Q2 a) Transpiration

b) i) 11.9 + 12.6 + 13.0 = 37.5

37.5 ÷ 3 = 12.5

Average = 12.5 cm moved in 5 minutes

12.5÷ = 5 = 2.5 cm per minute

Answer 2.5 cm per minute.

ii) The distance moved by the bubble would decrease because the transpiration rate would decrease, because the evaporation of water from the stomata would be slower.

iii) The rate of photosynthesis would decrease, so fewer stomata would be open and the rate of water loss would decrease, so the distance moved by the bubble would decrease.

c) The hairs on the leaf surface trap a layer of still, moist air close to the leaf surface. This would reduce evaporation of water from the leaf surface.

Q3 a) Blood in the capillary arriving in at the alveolus has a low concentration of oxygen. The oxygen concentration in the alveolus is high, so oxygen diffuses downs its concentration gradient, from the alveolus into the capillary.

b) i) Oxygen difference = 13.3 – 5.3
= 8 units

Oxygen uptake = $\dfrac{120 \times 8}{0.1}$ = 9600

ii) It would decrease the oxygen update because the alveoli have a smaller surface area.

iii) Increasing the oxygen concentration of the air breathed in would help increase oxygen uptake, so the person with emphysema would feel less breathless.

Q4 a)

Percentage of base in DNA sample	Name of base
30	thymine (T)
20	guanine (G)
30	adenine (A)
20	cytosine (C)

b) 30% of 2000 = 600

c) The part of the human DNA that contains the gene for insulin is identified. Special enzymes are used to cut this gene out of the DNA. Different enzymes are used to cut open the DNA of a vector (e.g. a virus or a bacteria) and insert the insulin DNA into the gap. The vector is used to transfer the insulin DNA into the final host bacteria. These bacteria are fermented. They reproduce asexually, producing many identical copies, and the bacteria manufacture human insulin from the gene that has been inserted into its DNA.

Q1 **a)** iodine solution

b)

Food	Colour obtained	Starch present
bread	purple	yes
milk	brown	no

c) **i)** Dissolve the food substance in water and add an equal volume of Benedict's solution. Mix and warm gently.

ii) An orange/red precipitate would form.

iii) The colour intensity increases from yellow through orange to red, depending on the amount of glucose present.

Q2 **a)** To ensure that the conditions in the yeast culture are anaerobic.

b) Factor: Amount of yeast
How controlled: Weigh the amount of yeast so that the same amount is used in each experiment.

c) **i)** 55 + 54 + 53 = 163; 162 ÷ 3 = 54

ii) The rate of respiration increased with increasing temperature up to 50 °C, but decreased at higher temperatures.

iii) His predictions were partially correct. His prediction was correct for temperatures up to 50 °C, but he did not predict that the rate of respiration would be lower at temperatures above this.

iv) The yeast's enzymes would be denatured at this temperature.

d) The third reading at 60 °C is much lower than the other two readings

e) **i)** Modification: the carbon dioxide given off could be collected and the volume measured.

Explanation: Measuring the actual volume of gas given off would be more accurate than measuring the number of bubbles. Bubbles can vary in size.

ii) Taking measures at 5 degree intervals will give a smoother graph. Alternatively, you could look at the behaviour with lower temperatures, eg 5 °C.

Q3 The population of the plant in the two different areas could be recorded using a quadrat.

1. The plant to be studied must be clearly identified.

2. A quadrat is placed randomly on the ground in one study area. This can be done by throwing the quadrat gently over your shoulder.

3. The number of plants of the chosen species within the quadrat are counted.

4. Steps 2 and 3 are repeated at least 30 times, the results recorded and the average number of plants per quadrat calculated.

5. The whole process is repeated for the second study area. The two areas should be of similar size.

ANSWERS AND SOLUTIONS

Chapter 1 THE NATURE AND VARIETY OF LIVING ORGANISMS

Characteristics of living organisms (page 8)

Q1 Movement, respiration, sensitivity, growth, reproduction, excretion, nutrition.

Q2 Nutrition and respiration.

Variety of living organisms (page 11)

Q1 Plants have chloroplasts and can photosynthesise while animals cannot.

The cells of plants have walls but animal cells have only a membrane.

You might also have said that animals can usually move from one place to another while plants are often sedentary, or that many animals can coordinate their movement using nerves.

Q2 They cannot reproduce independently but need to infect the cells of another living organism to do so.

Q3 Animals and fungi.

Chapter 2 STRUCTURES AND FUNCTIONS IN LIVING ORGANISMS

Cell structure (page 16)

Q1 **a** It does not contain any chloroplasts (and therefore no chlorophyll).

Any green parts of a plant will contain chloroplasts.

b Onions grow underground, so they will not receive any light. There is no point in them having chloroplasts as they will not be able to photosynthesise.

By going into detail and mentioning photosynthesis you show clearly that you understand the reason.

c It has a cell wall, a large vacuole and a regular shape.

There are some exceptions, in that some plant cells may not have large vacuoles or a regular shape. But they all have a cell wall.

Q2 **a** Cell membrane.

Don't forget that everything that goes in or out of a cell goes through the membrane.

b Nucleus or chromosomes.

Both are correct. Chromosomes is a more specific answer and shows more understanding.

c Vacuole.

Don't forget that only plants have large vacuoles.

d Cell wall.

The membrane would simply burst if the cell became too big. The cell wall is more rigid and resists this.

Q3 The pigment chlorophyll in chloroplasts absorbs light energy (usually from the sun).

Biological molecules (page 19)

Q1 Carbon, hydrogen and oxygen.

Q2 The sample of food is mixed with ethanol. The liquid portion of the test mixture is poured off into a test tube or beaker of water. If lipid is present the water turns milky. The test works because lipids are soluble in ethanol but not in water.

Q3 At high temperatures enzymes are denatured and will not work.

Movement of substances into and out of cells (page 28)

Q1 The salt forms a very concentrated solution on the slug's surface so water leaves its body by osmosis.

This happens with slugs because their skin is partially permeable. It would not happen with us because our skin is not.

Q2 **a** Diffusion.

There is a lower concentration of carbon dioxide inside the leaf as it is continually being used up.

b Neither.

The food is squeezed along by muscles in the gullet.

c Neither.

Again, water is being forced out.

d Osmosis.

As the celery is dried up the cells contain very concentrated solutions.

Q3 To provide energy for the active transport of minerals like nitrates into the roots.

The concentration of minerals in soils is usually lower than the concentration of minerals in plant cells. Plants therefore can't rely on diffusion to get more of these minerals and must expend energy on actively 'pulling' them in.

Q4 Diffusion is the movement of particles from an area of higher concentration to an area of lower concentration. In active transport particles move against a concentration gradient. They move from an area of low concentration into an area of high concentration. Active transport requires energy from respiration. Examples of diffusion include: movement of oxygen from lungs into blood; movement of carbon dioxide from blood into oxygen; movement of glucose from villi in small intestines into blood. Examples of active transport include: the movement of minerals from the soil into the root hair.

Questions about active transport are restricted to Higher Tier exam papers. The important facts to include in your answer are:
• particles move against a concentration gradient;
• energy (from respiration) is needed.

Nutrition (page 41)

Q1 a Carbon dioxide from the air enters the leaves through the stomata. Water moves from the soil into the roots and up the stem to the leaves.

As plants cannot move around, their raw materials have to be readily available. Note that sunlight is not a raw material. It is the energy source that drives the chemical reaction.

b Being broad allows as much light as possible to be absorbed. Being thin allows carbon dioxide to quickly reach the photosynthesising cells.

There are exceptions to this principle.

Q2 a Proteins are too big to pass through the wall of the ileum, so they have to be broken down into the smaller amino acids.

Only molecules that are already small do not need to be digested.

b Physical digestion is simply breaking food into smaller pieces. This is a physical change. Chemical digestion breaks down larger molecules into smaller ones. This is a chemical change because new substances are formed.

Many students, if asked to describe digestion, lose marks because they do not describe the breakdown of molecules.

c They are denatured.

This means they change their shape irreversibly, and can not work. In an exam do not say that they are 'killed' because they were never alive.

d To neutralise the acid from the stomach, because the enzymes in the small intestine can not work at an acidic pH.

Many students think that stomach acid itself breaks down food. It is the fact that it allows enzymes in the stomach to work that is important.

Q3 a Ingestion is taking in food. Egestion is passing out the undigested remains. Excretion is getting rid of things we have made.

Many students lose marks because they confuse egestion and excretion. Passing out faeces is egestion. Getting rid of urea in urine or breathing out carbon dioxide are examples of excretion because these substances are made in the body.

b Ingestion: mouth. Egestion: anus.

Excretion occurs in various places.

Respiration (page 44)

Q1 To provide energy for life processes like movement and to generate warmth.

Don't give vague answers like 'to stay alive'. If a question in an exam has several marks then give the correct number of points in your answer.

Q2 In every cell of the body.

You could be even more specific and point out that respiration occurs in the cytoplasm or in the mitochondria. Many students confuse respiration and breathing, and would have said 'lungs'.

Q3 a Aerobic respiration provides more energy (for the same amount of glucose) and does not produce lactic acid (which will have to be broken down).

Given sufficient oxygen, respiration will be aerobic.

b If more energy is needed and the oxygen necessary cannot be provided.

Anaerobic respiration is not as efficient as aerobic respiration. It is only used as a 'top up' to aerobic respiration.

Gas exchange (page 51)

Q1 Leaves have stomata to allow gases to enter and leave. They are thin so that gases do not have far to travel.

Q2 **a** Just two, the wall of the alveolus and the wall of the blood capillary.

This short distance is important so gases can easily move between the alveoli and the blood. Another way of looking at it is that the short distance increases the concentration gradient.

b To ensure that oxygen rapidly diffuses from the area of high concentration, in the alveoli, to the area of low concentration, in the blood.

Don't forget that there is also a concentration gradient for carbon dioxide.

Q3 The diaphragm lowers and the ribcage moves upwards and outwards.

Both of these changes increase the volume of the thorax.

Q4 To keep them open to ensure that air can move freely.

This is particularly important because when the air pressure drops to take in more air from the outside this could otherwise make the air passages close in on themselves.

Transport (page 59)

Q1 **a** Xylem is made of dead cells. It carries water and minerals from the roots, up the stem, to the leaves. Phloem is made of living cells. It carries dissolved food substances from the leaves to other parts of the plant.

Make sure you can also identify the xylem and phloem in diagrams of sections of roots, stems and leaves.

Q2 Substances, for example oxygen, will quickly diffuse into the centre of a small organism. For larger organisms, diffusion would take too long so a transport system is needed to ensure quick movement of substances from one part of the organism to another.

Another way of explaining this is to say that smaller organisms have a larger surface area to volume ratio (or a larger surface relative to their size).

Q3 **a** In the lungs.

The blood arriving at the lungs contains little oxygen and is there to collect more.

b In respiring tissues around the body.

Every cell will need oxygen. Active cells like those in muscles will need most.

c To ensure that their bodies collect enough oxygen.

If the air contains less oxygen then less oxygen will enter the blood unless the body has some way of compensating.

Q4 **a** The ventricles pump the blood but the atria simply receive the blood before it enters the ventricles.

The ventricle walls contract and relax to squeeze out blood and take more in. This takes a lot of muscle. The atria, by comparison, do not need to squeeze as hard and must be easily inflated by the incoming low-pressure blood.

b The left ventricle has to pump blood around the whole body (apart from the lungs). The right ventricle 'only' sends blood to the lungs.

This is why your heart sounds louder on your left side.

Q5 **a** Veins have valves, thinner walls and a larger lumen.

The veins contain blood at a reduced pressure and are built so that they don't resist the flow of blood but rather help it on its way to the lungs.

b Capillary walls are permeable, allowing diffusion. Arteries and veins do not have permeable walls.

The arteries carry blood quickly to each organ or part of the body and the veins bring it back. The capillaries form a branching network inside organs.

Excretion (page 62)

Q1 The farmer will have been sweating to stay cool and so will have lost water this way. Unless the farmer has drunk a lot, his or her kidneys will have to reduce the amount of water that is lost as urine. This is why there is less. However, there will be just as much urea, so the urine is more concentrated and darker in colour.

The body has to lose extra water by sweating to maintain body temperature. Humans cannot reduce how much is lost in breathing as the lining of the alveoli in the lungs is always moist, nor can the amount lost in faeces be reduced greatly. The only way therefore to cut down on losses is to reduce urine output.

Q2 They remove carbon dioxide and water from the body.

Excretion is the removal of substances that have been produced in the body. Carbon dioxide is a waste product of respiration, as is some of the water.

Q3 The veins would have a lower concentration of salt and urea than the arteries. Also, as with any other organ, the oxygen level and blood pressure would be lower.

Although most other substances in the blood (e.g. glucose) are also initially filtered from the blood, most are the absorbed back before the blood leaves the kidneys. Also, don't forget that the arteries are carrying blood away from the heart into the kidneys, and the veins the reverse.

Coordination and response (page 73)

Q1 Auxin is no longer concentrated more on one side than the other, so one side does not grow more than the other.

Remember that growth in tropisms is by cell elongation, not the formation of new cells by cell division.

Q2 **a** A change, either in the surroundings or inside the body, that is detected by the body.

For example, if you were crossing a road and noticed a bus approaching the stimuli would have been the sight and sound of the bus.

b Receptors detect (sense) stimuli. The sense organs are receptors. Effectors are the parts of the body that respond. Effectors are usually muscles but can also be glands.

Some students get confused between effectors and the 'effects' that they produce.

Q3 In the nervous system, signals are sent very quickly as electro-chemical impulses along neurones and the effects of the signal usually last a short time. In the endocrine system signals are sent more slowly as hormones through the blood and the effects usually last longer.

Both of these systems are involved in co-ordination (responding to stimuli). Both are needed because of the different nature of their effects.

Chapter 3 REPRODUCTION AND INHERITANCE

Reproduction (page 84)

Q1 **a** In the testes.

b Growth spurts; hair growth on face and body; penis, testes and scrotum growth and development; sperm production; voice breaking; the body becoming broader and more muscular; sexual 'drive' development.

Q2 **a** Progesterone.

b From the corpus luteum (the remains of the follicle left in the ovary).

Q3 **a** Maternal and fetal blood do not mix.

b The fetus is cushioned inside a bag of amniotic fluid.

Inheritance (page 93)

Q1 **a** Eye colour, height, shape of face (there are other examples). These are genetic features and as they are identical twins they will have the same genes.

b Skin colour, accent, how muscular they are (there are other examples). These features are affected by the environment. They are doing different jobs in different climates, so their environments are different.

Some features like eye colour are purely genetically controlled and so will be identical. Some features like accent are purely environmentally controlled and so would probably differ. Many features, like skin colour, are controlled both by genes and the environment (i.e. tanning) so they would also show differences.

Q2 Chemical base, gene, chromosome, cell nucleus, cell.

Q3 Let R be the dominant allele for tongue rolling and r the recessive allele for not being able to roll your tongue.

If not being able to roll your tongue is a recessive condition then the 'non-roller' child

parents: **Rr**   **Rr**

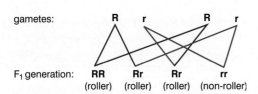

gametes: **R**   **r**   **R**   **r**

F₁ generation: **RR**   **Rr**   **Rr**   **rr**
           (roller) (roller) (roller) (non-roller)

must be rr. This means each parent must have at least one r allele. As the parents can roll their tongues they must therefore both be Rr.

Chapter 4 ECOLOGY AND THE ENVIRONMENT

The organism in the environment (page 97)

Q1 The average number of dandelions in 1 quadrat (1 m²) was 25 ÷ 10 = 2.5. The field is 200 m² so the total number of dandelions is 2.5 × 200 = 500.

You might have to do some maths so don't forget your calculator in your exam.

Q2 If the pupil in the previous question had only placed her quadrat where there were dandelions and had deliberately missed out those areas without any she would have calculated a much higher estimate.

Q3 An ecosystem is a community of different species of plants and animals in a particular environment that interrelate.

Feeding relationships (page 101)

Q1 a

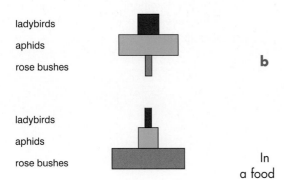

                          b

In a food chain where the producers are much larger than their consumers the pyramid of numbers is inverted. However, the pyramid of biomass is usually a normal pyramid shape.

Q2 Energy is lost at each stage of a food chain, so there is a limit as to how long a food chain can be.

Q3 Egestion and respiration.

Cycles within ecosystems (page 104)

Q1 a Photosynthesis

b Respiration and combustion.

Until the last few hundred years combustion played quite a small part in this. It is now playing a bigger role and this is the reason for the build up of carbon dioxide in the atmosphere.

Q2 This is the only way they can get the nitrogen they need.

The nitrogen is made available by digesting the protein in the insects' bodies.

Q3 Nitrifying bacteria produce nitrates from decayed remains. Denitrifying bacteria convert nitrates and other nitrogen compounds into nitrogen gas.

Denitrifying bacteria therefore have an opposite effect to nitrogen-fixing bacteria.

Human influences on the environment (page 109)

Q1 The greenhouse effect describes how some of the gases in the atmosphere restrict heat escaping from the Earth. Global warming is an increase in the Earth's temperature that may well be caused by an increased greenhouse effect.

Remember that it is the increased greenhouse effect that people are concerned about. A greenhouse effect is not only normal but essential for life on Earth.

Q2 This would increase their costs, which would have to be passed on to their customers, who might not want to pay more.

An added problem is that, unlike pollution into rivers, the problems caused by acid rain take place a long way from the source of the pollution.

Q3 Eutrophication is the overgrowth of plant life in water courses, especially algae, which reduces the oxygen available in the water and may cause the reduction of other species. It is caused by an excess of nutrients for plant growth which could be due to sewage or fertiliser pollution.

Chapter 5 USE OF BIOLOGICAL RESOURCES

Food production (page 118)

Q1 **a** To kill unwanted bacteria.

This question could be answered even if you have not studied about making yoghurt. The questions refer to your knowledge of bacteria and the stimulus material in the question.

b The bacteria will reproduce quickly.

The usefulness of bacteria is that they can reproduce very quickly by asexual reproduction.

c At 80°C the bacteria *L cto c llus* will be destroyed so lactic acid will not be released.

It does not matter that you have not heard of this bacterium before. It is your understanding of microorganisms and their ability to use the stimulus material that is being tested.

Q2 **a** The bacteria will reproduce quickly.

The first part of this question could be answered even if you have not studied about industrial fermenters. The questions refer to your knowledge of bacteria.

b Two from: bacteria divide asexually; offspring will be identical to their parents; an exact copy of genetic information is passed on each time.

The usefulness of bacteria is that they can reproduce very quickly by asexual reproduction. This allows identical offspring to be produced rapidly.

c Two from: penicillin; insulin; alcohol for fuel; most antibiotics.

Insulin and penicillin are the more specific answers. If you cannot remember these, then a general reference to antibiotics should gain marks.

Q3 Increased carbon dioxide allows for an increase in the rate of photosynthesis and thus and increase in growth rate.

Q4 Your answer could include diseases, parasites, nuisance fish, predators, silt, pesticides, chlorine, other chemicals.

Selective breeding (page 120)

Q1 Your answer could include: increased yield, disease resistance, resistance to adverse weather conditions.

Q2 Pick sheep with finer wool than the others. Breed these together. From the offspring pick those with the finest wool and breed these. Continue this over many generations.

The principle of selective breeding is the same whatever the example.

Genetic modification (page 122)

Q1 It refers to the way in which one base links to another, A to T and C to G, to connect the two strands of the molecule.

Q2 **a** Restriction enzymes.

b Ligase enzymes.

Q3 The term transgenic is used to describe an organism whose genetic material has been modified by the insertion of genetic material from another species.

Cloning (page 124)

Q1 Advantages: many roses with identical flowers can be produced relatively quickly. This would be useful if the roses on this particular plant sold well. Disadvantages: there is no variation, so if one rose was attacked by a plant disease then all the rest would be susceptible too.

The key point about cloning is that the new plants are genetically identical. This may or may not be an advantage.

Q2 The nucleus of a cell from a sheep's udder. This was possible because the nuclei of all cells contain a full set of chromosomes.

Q3 Transgenic animals could be used to produce large quantities of biological products of use to humans, e.g. antibodies to treat disease or organs for transplantation.

GLOSSARY

Adaptation

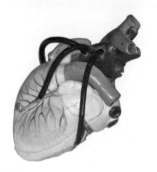

Artery

Auxin

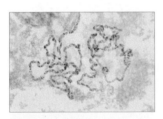

Chromosomes

Conservation

absorption the movement of digested food molecules from the gut into the blood stream

active transport movement of molecules across a cell membrane using energy from respiration; movement is often against a concentration gradient

adaptation the features or characteristics of an organism that makes it suited to its particular environment

aerobic using oxygen

alimentary canal tubular part of the digestive system, from mouth to anus

allele one of two genetic instructions for a particular characteristics, one received from each parent (e.g. spotted coat and black coat are two alleles for coat colour in leopards)

anaerobic without oxygen; anaerobic respiration occurs when oxygen is not available

artery vessel that carries blood away from the heart

assimilation the process by which simple food molecules are made into complex molecules in the body

auxin plant hormone that stimulates growth in the growing tip

balanced diet intake of food that supplies all the protein, fat, carbohydrate, vitamins and minerals that the body needs in the right amounts

birth control methods used to prevent conception (e.g. condoms, contraceptive pill)

capillaries tiny blood vessels in the tissues; every cell in the body is in very close proximity to a capillary; enabling gaseous exchange

carbon cycle a scheme that shows how the essential element carbon is used, created and recycled in nature

cell the 'building blocks' of which tissues are composed; some microorganisms are just one cell

chromosomes the structures in the nucleus that contain the DNA

clone a genetically identical copy

competition battle between organisms that live in the same place for the resources that are available

concentration gradient the difference in the amount of a substance between two areas; diffusion is usually along the concentration gradient: molecules move from the area of high concentration to the area of low concentration

conservation the processes of protecting an environment or habitat from change, so that the natural state is maintained and the organisms that live there can flourish

consumer (primary/secondary) animal in a food web; primary consumers eat plants; secondary consumers eat primary consumers

dialysis a technique used to filter the blood artificially if the kidneys do not function adequately

diffusion net movement of molecules along a concentration gradient; it is a passive process (it does not use energy)

digestion break-down of food; mechanical digestion breaks food down into smaller pieces (e.g. by chewing and the muscular action of the stomach) ready for chemical digestion by enzymes

DNA the molecule that carries genetic information in genes

dominant allele the allele that is expressed in the phenotype (e.g. spotted coat in leopards)

dormant in a suspended state; seeds stay dormant until conditions are right for germination

ecosystem a community of organisms of different species that live together in a particular area and interact with each other and that environment

effector part of the body that brings about a response to a stimulus

egestion removal of undigested material from the body (faeces) (compare with excretion)

enzyme a protein that acts as a catalyst, speeding up reactions in the body

eutrophication a process that severely damages water ecosystems: nitrates in fertilisers run into water and cause growth of algae, which causes plants to die because they do not get light to photosynthesise, and fish and other organisms die due to lack of oxygen

evolution adaptation (change) of organisms over time to changes in their environment through the process of natural selection

excretion removal of waste substances that have been generated by the body (compare with egestion)

fertilisation fusion (joining) of male and female sex cells

flaccid plants become flaccid (floppy) when they lose water by osmosis and the vacuole shrinks and does not push against the cell wall to give the plant support

food chain/web diagram showing the flow of energy between organisms; a food chain is a simple 'line' (plant, primary consumer, secondary consumer); food webs are a combination of food chains

gaseous exchange in the tissues, diffusion of oxygen from blood into cells and of carbon dioxide from cells into blood; the reverse occurs in the lungs

gene a piece of DNA that is the code for one instruction

genetic engineering chemical manipulation of genes

genetically modified plants or animals that have had a gene from another species introduced, e.g. to make a plant resistant to a virus

Dominant allele

Ecosystem

Effector

Fertilisation

Gene

Genetically modified

Microbes

Nutrition

Organism

Oxygen debt

genotype description of the two alleles for a particular characteristic

germination start of plant growth from a seed, which only occurs when there is the right amount of light and water and an appropriate temperature

homeostasis the maintenance of a constant internal environment in the body (e.g. constant temperature, water balance, etc.)

hormone a chemical that is released from a gland and travels in the blood to another site in the body (its target organ), where it has its effect; hormones are described as chemical messengers

inherited passed on from parent to offspring via the genes

key a system used for identifying an organism by asking a series of linked questions

limiting factor a factor (e.g. light, temperature) that controls the rate of photosynthesis; it is the condition that is least favourable

meiosis the process of cell division that occurs to make gametes (eggs, sperm, pollen cells); the number of chromosomes is halved

menstrual cycle the continuous sequence of events in a woman's reproductive organs; each cycle of ovulation (ripening and release of an egg) and menstruation (shedding of the unwanted uterus lining) takes about 28 days and is controlled by a number of hormones

microbes (microorganisms) tiny, usually single-celled, organism (e.g. bacteria) that cause disease

mitosis the process of cell division that produces identical copies of the cell

mutation a change in the structure of DNA

natural selection the key process of evolution: the organisms that are best suited to the environment are the ones that survive and reproduce

negative feedback a key mechanism by which homeostasis is achieved; the body monitors its internal environment and reacts by trying to reduce any changes that occur, back to the normal level

neurone a single nerve cell, many of which together form a nerve

nitrogen cycle a scheme that shows how nitrogen is used, released and recycled in nature

nutrition the process by which an organism gets the chemicals and energy it needs (nutrients) from its surroundings

organ a collection of tissues that together have a particular function (e.g. the kidney)

organism a living thing, ranging in size from a single-celled microorganism to an elephant

osmosis movement of water molecules through a partially permeable membrane, from a weak solution to a stronger solution

oxygen debt the result of anaerobic respiration; extra oxygen is needed after exercise to break down the lactic acid formed during anaerobic respiration

partially permeable description of a membrane (e.g. the cell membrane) that has tiny pores (holes) which allow some molecules (e.g. water) but not larger molecules to pass through

peristalsis the rhythmic muscular contractions of the stomach and intestine that move food along the alimentary canal

phenotype the apparent result of gene expression (e.g. black coat in leopards)

photosynthesis the chemical process in which plants absorb UV light and carbon dioxide and create glucose and oxygen

pollution contamination of land or water with undesirable material (e.g. chemicals or sewage)

population group of organisms of the same species living in a particular area

receptor a structure that detects information about the environment (e.g. heat)

recessive allele the allele that is not expressed in a phenotype unless there are two copies

reflex arc the pathway along which nerve impulses travel during a simple reflex (such as withdrawing your hand from a hot object)

reproduction (asexual/sexual) process of creating new members of a species; asexual reproduction does not involve sex cells; sexual reproduction is the combination of sex cells

respiration the chemical process by which cells generate energy by breaking down glucose

selective breeding a way of trying to introduce favourable characteristics into animals or plants by choosing which ones to breed with

specialisation the process by which cells have developed (often in terms of structure) to perform a particular function more efficiently

tissue a collection of similar cells that work together to achieve a particular function; several different tissues make up an organ

translocation movement of dissolved sugars and other molecules through a plant

transpiration evaporation of water vapour from the surface of a plant

tropism growth response to a particular stimulus in plants

turgid plant cells that are turgid have a full vacuole and the cytoplasm pushes against the cell wall, giving the plant structure and support

variation (continuous/discontinuous) differences between organisms; continuous variation describes features that can have any value (e.g. height); discontinuous variation describes characteristics that have only a particular number of possibilities (e.g. eye colour, fur colour, sex)

vein blood vessel that carries blood to the heart

water potential the capacity of a plant cell to take up water by osmosis; a turgid cell cannot take up any more water and thus has no water potential

Photosynthesist

Pollution

Receptor

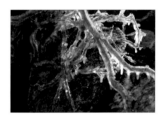
Tropism

Water potential

INDEX